KU-681-220

UNDERSTANDING TEACHING
Continuity and change in teachers' knowledge

William Louden

CASSELL

TEACHERS
COLLEGE
PRESS

Teachers College,
Columbia University
New York

For Susan, who makes all the difference

First published 1991 by
Cassell Educational Limited
Villiers House
41/47 Strand
London WC2N 5JE
England

Published in the United States of America by
Teachers College Press
Columbia University
New York, NY 10027
USA

© Cassell Educational Limited 1991

All rights reserved. No part of this publication may be reproduced
or transmitted in any form or by any means, electronic or
mechanical including photocopying, recording or any information
storage or retrieval system, without prior permission in writing
from the publishers.

British Library Cataloguing in Publication Data
Louden, William
    Understanding teaching: continuity and change in teachers'
    knowledge. – (Teacher development).
    1. Teaching
    I. Title   II. Series
    317.102

ISBN 0-304-32345-4 (hardback)
        0-304-32346-2 (paperback)

Library of Congress Cataloging-in-Publication Data
Louden, William.
    Understanding teaching: continuity and change in teachers'
    knowledge / William Louden.
        p.   cm.
    Includes bibliographical references (p.   ) and index.
    ISBN 0-8077-3102-1. – ISBN 0-8077-3101-3 (pbk.)
    1. Teaching – Case studies.   2. Teachers – Canada –
    Case studies.
    3. Education, Secondary – Canada – Case studies.   I. Title.
    LB1025.2.L655   1991
    371.1′02 – dc20
                                                90-24708
                                                    CIP

Typeset by Colset Private Limited, Singapore
Printed and bound in Great Britain by
Biddles Ltd, Guildford and King's Lynn

Contents

Foreword

In Britain and Australia, they call it teaching. In the United States and Canada, they call it instruction. Whatever terms we use, we have come to realize in recent years that the teacher is the ultimate key to educational change and school improvement. The restructuring of schools, the composition of national and provincial curricula, the development of bench-mark assessments – all these things are of little value if they do not take the teacher into account. Teachers don't merely deliver the curriculum. They develop, define it and reinterpret it too. It is what teachers think, what teachers believe and what teachers do at the level of the classroom that ultimately shapes the kind of learning that young people get. Growing appreciation of this fact is placing working with teachers and understanding teaching at the top of our research and improvement agendas.

For some reformers, improving teaching is mainly a matter of developing better teaching methods, of improving instruction. Training teachers in new classroom management skills, in active learning, co-operative learning, one-to-one counselling and the like is the main priority. These things are important, but we are also increasingly coming to understand that developing teachers and improving their teaching involves more than giving them new tricks. We are beginning to recognize that, for teachers, what goes on inside the classroom is closely related to what goes on outside it. The quality, range and flexibility of teachers' classroom work is closely tied up with their professional growth — with the way that they develop as people and as professionals.

Teachers teach in the way they do not just because of the skills they have or have not learned. The ways they teach are also grounded in their backgrounds, their biographies, in the kinds of teachers they have become. Their careers – their hopes and dreams, their opportunities and aspirations, or the frustration of these things — are also important for teachers' commitment, enthusiasm and morale. So too are relationships with their colleagues – either as supportive communities who work together in pursuit of common goals and continuous improvement, or as individuals working in isolation, with the insecurities that sometimes brings.

As we are coming to understand these wider aspects of teaching and teacher development, we are also beginning to recognize that much more than pedagogy, instruction or teaching method is at stake. Teacher development, teachers' careers, teachers' relations with their colleagues, the conditions of status, reward and leadership under which they work – all these affect the quality of what they do in the classroom.

This international series on *Teacher Development* brings together some of the very best current research and writing on these aspects of teachers' lives and work. The books in the series seek to understand the wider dimensions of teachers' work, the depth of teachers' knowledge and the resources of biography and experience on which it draws, the ways that teachers' work roles and responsibilities are changing as we restructure our schools, and so forth. In this sense, the books in the series are written for those who are involved in research on teaching, those who work in initial and in-service teacher education, those who lead and administer teachers, those who work with teachers and, not least, teachers themselves.

Bill Louden's first book, *Understanding Teaching*, gives us a beautifully reflective and richly described close-up view of the teacher's world. Louden is an experienced researcher, teacher and educational administrator. Yet what his study shows is not the arrogance of preconceived intellectual wisdom but the humility, insight and understanding that come from studying and working intensively in a collaborative relationship with one teacher. Louden shows us what is to be learned from working with teachers in this kind of depth. By implication, he shows us how little we know about teachers and teaching when we research them or work with them or administer them in more fleeting, superficial ways.

Louden's elegantly written study provides us with a powerful sense and feeling of what it is like to be a teacher, to be this teacher. But through this study we not only learn about this teacher, we come to learn things that may apply more generally. Louden makes a significant contribution to our understanding of reflection, of how teachers actually do (not merely how they should) reflect on their work. He highlights the impact of biographical influences on teachers and the way they approach their work. Because of this, because of the deeply personal nature of much teaching, he alerts us to the likely reality for most teachers: that, for them, meaningful and lasting change is likely to be slow. In an administrative and political world hooked on change, Louden brings us back to the importance to teachers of continuity and traditions. Louden's book is one that understands the teacher from the inside out. Anyone interested in working with teachers in that way will find it a valuable source of insight and reflection.

Andy Hargreaves
Ontario Institute for Studies in Education, Toronto

Preface

The irony of a case study such as this is that the debt of gratitude I owe to the teacher we called 'Johanna' cannot be acknowledged by name. This was a collaborative study and it took shape through the experiences we shared. Although I remain finally responsible for the interpretations which appear in this text, Johanna shared with me the journey which led to these interpretations. She took the terrible risk of inviting me into her classroom, spent countless hours talking with me about the meaning of her work, and read every word I wrote. More than any of this she became my friend, invited my family to share the events and celebrations which mark out her year, and made our stay in Canada much richer than it might have been. Like Johanna, the principal, staff and students of Community School were generous in their support of my study and made the experience of field work pleasant and rewarding.

I am also grateful to the Ministry of Education of Western Australia and the Ontario Institute for Studies in Education for financial assistance which made this research possible. The Chair of my PhD thesis committee, Joel Weiss, helped me frame this project, helped me make some good decisions and avoid some bad ones, and was unfailingly enthusiastic and supportive of my work. Brent Kilbourn and Andy Hargreaves, the other members of my committee, were generous with their time, energy and ideas and made the thesis committee meetings a particular pleasure. The impetus and the opportunity to reshape the thesis into its current form came from Andy Hargreaves. I am particularly appreciative of the efforts he made to bridge the gap of space and time while I prepared this manuscript.

William Louden
Perth, Australia

Introduction

The fatal flaw in most programmes for the improvement of teaching is a fundamental misunderstanding about teachers and their work. Whether proposals for instructional improvement come from the educational right wing or the educational left, they share the assumption that the key to improvement is some better way of teaching. Unfortunately, the graveyard of educational reform is littered with better ways that did not appeal to teachers: open-plan buildings that did not lead to open education; heuristic syllabuses that decayed into lists of content to be learned; and principles of effective teaching that made more sense to researchers than to practitioners.[1] The argument of this book is that it is not enough to remove the walls, to provide a syllabus which favours process over products, or to identify key characteristics of effective teaching. What is required is to pay close attention to the meaning teachers make of the walls, the syllabus or particular teaching practices. Before proposing a change, we must learn to ask, 'How does this change relate to these teachers' understanding of their work?'

This study offers three points of departure from previous studies of teachers' knowledge: a new approach to the problem of understanding teaching; an analysis of the role of reflection in changes in teachers' knowledge and action; and an appreciation of the place of continuity and tradition in understanding teachers' work.

UNDERSTANDING TEACHING

The largest body of research which attempts to understand the meaning teachers make of their work is research on teachers' thinking. This research focuses on the thinking, planning and theorizing teachers do outside the classroom (see Clark and Peterson, 1986). Research on teachers' thinking has been supplemented by ethnographic description of their routines, rules and patterns of teaching (see Leinhardt *et al.*, 1987, for example). In addition, there is a growing school of research which focuses on the influence of biography on teachers' understanding of their work (Connelly and Clandinin, 1988; Butt and Raymond, 1987). This book brings together all three strands of enquiry. Through an intensive case study of one teacher's planning, her classroom teaching, and the biographical context she brings to her work, this study provides a classroom perspective on the knowledge teachers have and use.

Johanna, the teacher whose work is described in this book, teaches art, music and drama in a small Canadian, public (state-maintained) school for students aged 12 and 13. My account of Johanna's work begins with a biographical introduction and a description of her skilful, routine practice. Building on this description of her teaching, the study follows Johanna through two cycles of change. First, it follows her as she taught a series of writing lessons. The new patterns of teaching she needed to learn were consistent with her previous goals and teaching practices, and the gaps in understanding she confronted were small and easily crossed. When she tried to teach science, however, she was uncomfortable with the goals of the syllabus and unable to reshape her previous patterns of teaching in order to achieve these goals. The gap was too great to cross, and Johanna could not find a way of teaching the syllabus while remaining consistent with what she already understood about teaching.

The bulk of this book concerns the lessons Johanna and I taught and the conversations we had about them. Interwoven with this description, and emerging from my commentary on her work, is an alternative approach to the problem of understanding teaching. From a practitioner's perspective, I argue, teaching is a struggle to discover and maintain a settled practice, a set of routines and patterns of action which resolve the problems posed by particular subjects and groups of children. These patterns, content and resolutions to familiar classroom problems are shaped by each teacher's biography and professional experience. The meaning of these patterns of action only becomes clear when they are set in the context of a teacher's personal and professional history, her hopes and dreams for teaching, and the school in which she works. A teacher's response to new problems is shaped by these historically sedimented patterns of action. Following the hermeneutic philosopher Hans-Georg Gadamer (1975), I have called this predisposition a *horizon* of understanding. Such horizons of understanding are not static, but are constantly in the process of formation. Confronted by new problems and challenges, a teacher struggles to resolve them in ways that are consistent with the understanding she brings to the problem and this process leads, in turn, to new horizons of understanding about teaching.

REFLECTION AND CHANGE

Patterns of teaching developed in an attempt to reduce the uncertainty of life in classrooms may tend to solidify into an unchanging routine, but classrooms also continue to provide surprising situations. In these situations, to use Dewey's terms, reflective action may replace routine action (Dewey, 1933). The value of reflection has long been recognized in education, and has become an important theme in teacher education and teacher development in the years since Donald Schon's influential work on reflective practice (Schon, 1983, 1987). One of the weaknesses in the educational literature, however, has been the emphasis on prescription rather than description. There is universal agreement that reflection is a good thing for teachers, and considerable interest in elaboration of various versions of the concept, but rather less empirical exploration of the kinds of reflection teachers are able to do in their day-to-day work.[2]

As this study follows Johanna learning to teach writing and science, it documents an enormous range and volume of reflection. Building on the distinction between reflection-in-action and reflection-on-action (Schon, 1983), and Habermas's (1971) distinction between the technical, practical and critical interests of reflection, I go on to develop a conceptual account of the range of her reflection in terms of a series of *forms* and *interests* of reflection.

CONTINUITY AND TRADITION

The third and final theme of this study is the relationship between teachers' horizons of understanding and their reflection. Teachers can and do want to change, but the possibilities for change are shaped by their horizons of understanding and by the traditions of teaching within which they work. My purpose here is to rehabilitate the concept of continuity, and to argue that educational reform is best approached by exploring change from the teachers' perspective.

The failure of educational reform has often been blamed on teachers. Teachers are widely regarded as unreflective, conservative, narrow-minded, and more inclined to accept unfavourable conditions than to struggle to change them. Such supposed character traits are as familiar to readers of the standard works on teachers as they are to disappointed reformers.[3] However, as Willard Waller pointed out as long ago as 1932, teachers' unwillingness to change is often improperly dismissed as resistance:

> Most of the programs for the rehabilitation of the schools founder on the rock of teacher resistance. For the most part, we consider this resistance well placed. The common-sense understanding which teachers have of their problems bites deeper than do the maunderings of most theorists. Teachers will do well to insist that any program of educational reform shall start with them, that it shall be based on, and shall include, their common-sense insight. (Waller, 1932, p. 457)

One of the implications of the understanding of teaching advanced in this book is that more attention should be paid to the forces for continuity in teachers' work. Johanna's common-sense understanding, her repertoire of safe and familiar practices, is what allows her to overcome the most common problems she faces. More than this, as I suggested earlier, her practice is deeply connected to her biography and her hopes and dreams for teaching. To teach the School Board's science syllabus required more than mastering new content; it required a significant change in her current horizons of understanding about teaching. In order to teach the syllabus as it was intended, she would have had to put aside familiar patterns of teaching built up over years, disturb the careful balance between her educational goals and problems of classroom management, and add new lessons and strategies to her repertoire.

The horizons of understanding which enabled Johanna to learn more about teaching writing and inhibited her from teaching science according to the syllabus are not just personal and idiosyncratic, because her understanding of teaching is constructed within larger frames of reference. Following Blyth (1965), I have called these frames of reference *traditions*: similar ways of understanding teaching which are shared by groups which may be separated by thousands of miles.

These broad understandings of teaching include traditions shared by alternative teachers, progressive teachers, teachers of art and crafts, and teachers in middle schools. The impact of these invisible communities of intersubjective agreement, and the living traditions in every school, is to support further the power of continuity in teachers' practice.

The combination of teachers' personal horizons of understanding and the traditions within which these horizons are constructed promotes continuity rather than change. The power of the past in shaping the future has long been recognized in the professions which set out to deal with personal change. Indeed, it is the therapist's willingness to wait for clients to see the need for change that leads to the old joke: 'How many therapists does it take to change a light bulb?' 'Only one, but the light bulb has got to *want* to change.' Until those of us who look for improvement and change in education learn to approach teachers with more respect for the power of continuity in their work, we are likely to continue to be disappointed with the progress of educational reform.

A NOTE ON METHOD

This study is based on a period of intensive fieldwork in Johanna's school.[4] During a year of involvement with Community School, from February 1988 to February 1989, I made notes about 65 visits to the school and meetings with the teachers, 44 of which were in an intensive period of participant observation from September to December 1988. At the end of each meeting or day in the school I wrote narrative field notes about my experience, entering them directly on to computer files. As the study was a participant-observation study and my commitment was to try to understand events by participating in them, I made no attempt to scratch down notes *during* the days at Community School. I did not want to make my hosts nervous by making notes in front of them, or to engage in an ethnographic dash to the washroom to make notes in private, so in the early months of the study I relied solely on my memory at the end of the day for notes. After a time, I realized that my notes from memory lacked that quality journalists call 'actuality', the actual words spoken by participants. As I was by then a well-established member of the school community, I was able to negotiate permission to use a micro-cassette recorder to tape lessons, small group discussions and lunchtime conversations. I used these tapes as a supplement to my memory of the day's events, and wove quotations from them into the narrative field notes I made at the end of each day. Occasionally, when a conversation or lesson seemed particularly useful, I transcribed the complete audio-tape.

In producing these notes I tried to be concrete, providing details of action and refraining from deliberate interpretation as far as possible. The notes followed the time sequence of events, and I wrote down everything I could remember at the end of the day. When I came to prepare the text of this study, I reshaped the field notes into stories. I began by selecting pieces from the field notes which seemed rich in possibilities for interpretation. Next, I eliminated details which interrupted the flow of the story I had chosen to tell, and then considered how clearly the story had emerged. Where necessary, I added details to make the context clearer to other readers.

In simple terms, that was the method of enquiry. Collected together and arranged to make an argument, these stories form the basis of this book.[5] Behind this method, however, stands my own sense of what it means to *understand* experience through disciplined enquiry. The notion of understanding which infuses this study is drawn from hermeneutic philosophy. One of several ideas I have drawn from Gadamer (1975) is that the rigour of a research method cannot guarantee the truth of research conclusions.[6] Like other postpositivist philosophers, Gadamer argues that there is no neutral foundation for understanding. Rather, understanding of events or texts is constructed through the preconceptions we bring to them. There is no prior state of understanding free of prejudices, and no method which can free us from the understanding we bring to each new experience. Prejudices, whether justified or not, are shaped by the authorities which provide the sources of our knowledge and the traditions which inform our ways of knowing (Gadamer, 1975, pp. 245–51). Understanding, therefore, is historical in that it is shaped by the traditions of understanding within which we make interpretations, and the preconceptions we carry forward to each act of interpretation.

This notion of understanding impels me to pay particular attention to the influence of history and tradition on other participants' understanding of events. For this reason, the study includes a biographical account of the case study teacher and explores the consequences of her biography and experience on her actions. Similarly, in so far as I have been aware of the influence of my own preconceptions I have attempted to declare them in the context of the events that are being described. More generally, I have taken the view that the meaning of events is not limited to the events themselves, but has a temporal quality. A full and vivid interpretation, I believe, requires attending to the meaning participants bring forward to events, and sufficiently extensive fieldwork to follow developments over time.

Understanding, however, remains elusive. Despite my attempts to provide stories based firmly on actual events, contextualized by the history of the participants and my own preconceptions, the text which emerges is still open to further interpretation. Understanding, as Gadamer puts it, is 'always more than the mere recreation of someone else's meaning' (Gadamer, 1975, p. 338). Understanding is in principle incomplete and continues to grow with each interpreter's encounter with new texts or experience. Always, it involves the creation of meaning from the text or experience in the light of the meaning-maker's preconceptions and the tradition of interpretation within which he or she acts. With each new reading of the same text, too, interpretations inevitably grow and change.

This inevitable gap between the researcher's final text and its readers implies that a text ought to be constructed in such a way that it is open to further interpretation. Thus this study generally deals with the case study evidence in large sections – stories – and where quotations or descriptions are taken out of context, the context is normally available elsewhere in the study. Moreover, the interpretive comments I make of the stories, with the benefit of the sweep of understanding of the completed study, are always separated from the stories themselves by a row of asterisks. Rather than resisting alternative interpretations, which studies constructed from brief and decontextualized quotations do, this study attempts to remain open to further interpretation.

NOTES

1. See Fullan (1982), Huberman and Miles (1984) and Kirst and Meister (1985).
2. See Connelly and Clandinin (1986a), Zeichner and Liston (1987), and Nolan and Huber (1989) for a representative range of approaches to reflection.

3. See Waller (1932), Jackson (1968) and Lortie (1975), for example.
4. Community School is a senior elementary school for students in Grades 7 and 8. Typically, these students are aged 12 and 13. In the United Kingdom, the school would be called a middle school. Elsewhere in North America it would be called a junior high school.
5. A comprehensive account of method and epistemology may be found in the PhD thesis on which this book is based (Louden, 1989).
6. Gadamer's major work is translated in English as *Truth and Method* (1975). See Weinsheimer (1985) for a book-length reading of this work. Gadamer's *Philosophical Hermeneutics* (1976), a collection of essays, provides several shorter and more approachable accounts of the ideas taken up in this study (see especially pp. 1–43).

Chapter 1

Johanna

HAROLD BRIDGES LIBRARY
S. MARTIN'S COLLEGE
LANCASTER

Community School is a public alternative school for children in Grades 7 and 8 (aged 12 and 13 years) housed in a large, squat, square, plain building on a small block of land in a residential neighbourhood in metropolitan Toronto. I first visited the school in the winter of 1988, while I was in the process of seeking an appropriate fieldwork site for this study. On that first day I was nervous and early, so I wandered around the snow-covered playground of the school, filling in time and wondering what the school would be like inside. Would I be welcome in the school? Would any of these teachers be interested in collaboration with a researcher? Would any of them be in the midst of the kinds of changes I was interested in documenting?

As soon as it was noon, I walked into the school and found the enquiry desk of Massey Public School, the elementary school which shared the building with Community School. I climbed the stairs to the third floor, and followed a brightly painted mural down the hallway past a series of closed classroom doors. I found the Community School office but it was empty. A bell rang, and two or three students drifted past, but there was no sign of a teacher. I spent perhaps ten minutes conspicuously inspecting the hallway notice-boards, which displayed cheerful snapshots of Community School students and teachers on school camps, and class photos of previous years. Eventually, I asked a likely looking student whether she knew where I could find Bob, the teacher I had made an appointment to see. The student didn't know and thought that he might have gone out to lunch, but offered to go looking for him. She disappeared through a set of double doors and when she returned she asked me to follow her. We entered a cluster of four open-area classrooms and she pointed out a teacher sitting at a desk surrounded by half a dozen boys holding sheets of paper which the teacher was inspecting and signing. Bob, the teacher, looked up and said that he was running behind time. I could see that he was busy, so I volunteered to wait for him in the hallway.

A few minutes later, Bob emerged from the classroom and welcomed me to the school. As we talked over lunch I introduced myself as a researcher and former teacher, interested in exploring the possibility of collaborative research with a teacher. Bob explained that there were four teachers at the school but only three present today. The fourth, Miles, was away at a school board–sponsored course about the new provincial English guidelines. Bob made a gently unfavourable remark about people outside schools taking teachers' time for 'in-service courses about methods that I have been using for twenty years'. In this case, he thought that the new guidelines would require no changes for teachers at Community School. Bob passed me some documents relating to the school's pro-gramme and explained that they usually began the year with a camp-ing trip organized by the students, which generally had the effect of making the school more cohesive. A teachers' strike at the beginning of the academic year had stopped them from running the camp and he thought that this had unfortunate consequences for the tone of the school. At some point during this conversation I mentioned that I was interested in the possibility of helping out around the school. This seemed to strike a responsive chord with Bob who said, 'We can always use an extra pair of hands.'

We were joined at the staffroom table by a second teacher, Johanna. Bob explained that they had taught together at another school years ago, and that he had tried to convince Johanna to join them when he and Freida had started Community School about seven years before. Johanna had finally joined the school at the beginning of the current academic year as a teacher of art, music and drama. Bob mentioned to Johanna that I was interested in helping out in some way at the school. I explained that I was interested in how students come to be independent learners and in the relationship between students' emotional states and their learning. Johanna was quick to say that they were 'the same thing'. Students could only learn when they were happy.

Throughout this conversation, there was a constant stream of students entering the staffroom, asking questions, joining teachers' conversations, or using the photocopier. When one of these students came in just as I was explaining why I was visiting the school, Johanna smiled and explained that part of working in the school was getting used to the interruptions. 'You learn to remember where you were in a conversation and take it up next time there's a chance', she said. Johanna stood up and helped a student look for something, then returned to our conversation.

For perhaps an hour and a half I sat at the table and talked to whichever teachers or students were there, getting the feel of the place and offering them an opportunity to decide whether they would be comfortable to have me around. Later, I visited the open-area classrooms several times, looking at the layout and facilities and chatting with the students. All but 12 of the 70 or so students at the school were out on their usual Thursday afternoon independent field trip. I felt quite awkward, especially at the beginning, and tended to look rather than participate. I had not been inside a classroom for a year, and it was five years since I had a class of my own. As the day drew to a close I waited for an opportunity to make some kind of interim arrangement with the teachers about permission to visit the school again. Before I had found an opportunity, Johanna asked whether I was interested in coming back. She reminded me that I had said I'd like to 'help out in some way', and asked me in what ways I would like to help out. Was I interested in the arts, for example? I explained that my background was as an English teacher with a particular interest in writing. I arranged to take part in Bob's Monday afternoon writing class and Johanna's Friday morning evaluation class. In both cases, it seemed that an extra pair of hands would be useful. Freida warned me that I might find the students a little difficult. Johanna protested, but Freida named a series of difficulties there had been with part-time or substitute teachers. My response was that it might be different for me, as I was looking to be a helper rather than a teacher.

As I left the school I felt very pleased. I had found a school with the sort of friendly and informal environment I had always admired. The three teachers I had met were pleasant and interesting – and willing to have me spend some time in the school – and I had really enjoyed being around students again. When I had time to read the promotional material about Community School, I realized that there was a close match between my own interests in education and Community School's vision of itself: a school for students who wished to become responsible for their own learning and take their place in a community

3

of learners, staffed by teachers who worked as a team and paid particular attention to the emotional and social needs of adolescents.

CIRCLING AROUND EACH OTHER

It took me another five visits before I felt confident enough to begin talking to any of the teachers about the possibility of participating in the study I was planning. Gradually, I had begun to think of Johanna as the most appropriate collaborator in the school. I am not sure whether she chose me or I chose her, but it transpired that she and I agreed to work together. This decision was preceded by a brief period of circling around each other, each time revealing more about ourselves and how we felt about Community School. This had already begun during my first visit, when she had asked me whether I was interested in coming back, and what ways I thought I might help out around the school.

The second step in this process was at the end of my next visit to the school (2 March, 1988). During the afternoon, many of the students had 'independent time' in the four-room open-area classroom. There was a lot happening: about 20 students were playing 'Go' or chess in Miles's room, with Miles and a visiting helper participating; half-a-dozen girls were at band practice with an itinerant music teacher; several Grade 7 boys were copying notes about science into their notebooks; three or four Grade 8 girls were sitting squeezed into a doorway discussing a very private matter about cliques among their peers; three Grade 8 boys were working at the computers, one was playing with graphics programs and two were entering a long and complex set of changes to a bulletin-board program; several boys were preparing their independent field trips for the next day; and three Grade 8 girls were sitting together reading fiction. All this activity was taking place against a background of noise created by the minority of students who were using independent time to chat, play and roam around the room.

At the end of the day I dropped into Johanna's room, a separate art room some distance from the open-area classroom, where she and several students were finishing cleaning up. She asked me how things had been out in the open area. I was surprised to hear myself say that some of the students had been 'wriggling around like maggots in a shoe box'. This response was less neutral than I intended. I was concerned that I would be misunderstood as disapproving of the school, so I went on to say that her room seemed quite different from the other classrooms. It was very orderly, with art stools neatly upturned on the desks, and the room was filled with students' work on display. Johanna said that she knew what I meant and had sometimes felt the same when she first arrived at the school. She went on to explain that she had found it hard to work in the open area, where students would come and go from her class at will, and so she had moved to this closed space of her own.

Half an hour later, after talking to Bob about the writing lesson which I had visited earlier in the afternoon, I was walking down the hallway past Johanna's classroom on my way out of the school. I decided on impulse to drop into Johanna's room again to say goodnight. She was sitting at her desk marking. We talked for a while about what it was like for me to try to reconstruct the meaning of what was happening in the school. As we talked about this issue, I took the opportunity to show her the notes I had made in my first five visits. I had been carrying a print-out of my field notes, in the hope that I would have an opportunity to give the teachers some sense of what I was making of the experience and of what sort of notes I was keeping. Johanna seemed surprised at how detailed the notes were and was interested in reading some of them. She read four or five pages, and then began to talk about her feelings about the direction in which the school was going. Principally, she thought that people needed to be clearer about the goals of the school. If she were to stay at Community School the next year, she said she would want the staff to meet and talk about their goals and the ways they went about achieving them. She mentioned that there was an outside facilitator at the school board whom she would like to invite to a 'Professional Activity' day in order to help staff work on the problem, and she also thought that my observations could be useful to the process. What I thought at the time, but did not say, was that I would be very reluctant to get caught in the cross-fire about the goals of the school. I was, however, encouraged that she thought I might be of some use because I recognized this as a step towards having something to trade for participation in my study.

Before my next visit, the following Monday (7 March), I had

made no arrangement to visit any particular teacher's class. As usual, I sat at the staffroom table before school and joined in the early morning coffee and gossip. I was surprised, and pleased, when Johanna asked who I was going to join today. I decided to go with her. When we arrived in her room there were six or eight students already working.

At the beginning of her lesson, Johanna organized several activities. Some students, who had not been tested for this term's guitar grade, were to be tested. Some were to complete artwork which was due, and others were working on the first of next term's art projects. Several students were completing their answers to questions about a school excursion. Johanna showed the class an attractive book of artwork using Plasticine and indicated that one of the options for art next term would be to produce some similar pieces of art. As other students began work Johanna handed out Plasticine to several boys who wanted to begin that project. For the remainder of the lesson, I sat with a group of students who were working on a lithograph, one of next term's art activities, while Johanna tested several students' guitar skills. As two of the students sitting at the table prepared for their guitar test, the others helped them. The students seemed to treat each other with respect, even those whose musical abilities were less developed than their own. This struck me as unusual for a group of this age, and I took it as an indication of the school's success in creating a supportive learning environment.

Later in the afternoon, I accompanied Johanna as she walked with a group of Grade 7 students to a swimming-pool a few blocks away. Once the students had begun their lesson with the swimming instructor, Johanna told me about her reaction to the notes I had showed her last time. She had been surprised at their detail and felt too closely observed. She was not sure that she wanted what she characterized as 'mistakes' to be recorded and written about. I explained that I had made an effort to limit my judgements, and she replied that the selection of things to include in the notes itself constituted a judgement. Johanna seemed quite guarded about what she was prepared to say. She commented that she felt more cautious being around me now that she realized how detailed were the notes about my visits to the school.

We sat in the sun by the edge of the pool for the next half-hour, swapping stories about research and teaching. Johanna expressed some reservations about the organization of Community School, and about the risk of participating in a research project such as this one. When I spoke to Johanna the next day (8 March, 1988) she began by saying that she had given very serious thought to whether or not she was willing to participate. On the one hand, she felt that it was risky having someone watching her and writing about her work. She felt uncomfortable that the 'mistakes' she made in a learning period would be recorded for posterity. On the other hand, she had always thought a lot about her work and welcomed the opportunity to have someone to talk to about it. She was finding the experience of teaching in this school very demanding, was spending a lot of time thinking about her work, and was looking for new ways of working with students. In view of the risks involved, she wanted to be sure that she and I shared some of the same values about teaching, so she asked me to give an account of myself.

I talked about my ambivalence about the use of authority in the classroom. As a teacher, I had always attempted to lead students towards independent learning, towards setting their own tasks and monitoring their own progress. Ironically, however, I had found it necessary to exercise a lot of authority while I taught students the classroom routines which enabled them to work with this apparent independence. Consequently, I wondered whether I had really taught students to work independently, or whether they were rats running in a different maze.

Johanna also wanted me to explain how I came to be at Community School, and how I had chosen her as a possible research collaborator. Her recollection was that I had just appeared in the staffroom one lunch-time. I explained that I had been looking for a suitable fieldwork site for some time and that the school had been recommended to me by a colleague whose daughter had recently attended Community School. I went on to explain in more detail what I had been looking for when I came to the school – a teacher who shared my interest in the balance between students' independence and teachers' control, who was struggling to make some changes in her teaching, and who was teaching subjects I did not know how to teach. Johanna's comment was that I had been lucky: she was concerned about these issues in her teaching, and she was in the middle of some difficult changes. It sounded to her as if I had found just the sort of teacher I was looking for. The match was so good that she was surprised I didn't arrive with a dozen roses!

During the next few months, I continued to visit Community School, discussed the details of my research proposal with Johanna and her principal, and interviewed Johanna. This biographical material appears in two parts in this chapter. The first, 'Johanna's Story' is a first-person account of her life as a student and a teacher. The second part is my interpretation of Johanna's story, drawing out a series of issues. Before turning to her story, however, I make some brief comments on research method and ethics. Johanna and I have both had a hand in the construction of 'Johanna's Story'. I made the occasion for the interviews, asked certain questions and provided an audience for her storytelling. She chose what she thought was important and what she was willing to share with me and with a wider audience. As such, the following story is just one of the stories she could have chosen to tell, and is shaped by her unfolding understanding of her life. Although it is presented in Johanna's own language and in her own rhythms of speech, I have edited and shaped the story in several ways, as I describe below.

The technical details of the construction of 'Johanna's Story' are that I interviewed Johanna at her home twice, on 28 July and 9 August, 1988, and prepared 52 pages of typed transcript. In addition, Johanna gave me a copy of an autobiographical piece she had written several years before in a summer-school course. I merged these two written texts, selecting anecdotes which seemed to throw some light on Johanna's development as a teacher. Many of the anecdotes have been condensed, and I have added linking sentences, deleted the repetitions and circumlocutions which characterize all of our oral language, and occasionally chosen a more tactful form of words. Thus, the text of 'Johanna's Story' follows the shape, language and rhythms of the stories she told me, but is not a literal transcription of the interviews which were its main source.

Like all other descriptions of Johanna and her work, early versions of this material were passed on to Johanna for correction and comment. Subsequently, we agreed to alter or omit certain details that she had mentioned in the interviews. Some details were judged to be too personal to make public; others concerned third parties who had not been, or could not be, consulted. Behind these minor amendments to the story she had first told stand a series of other stories she might have told: stories that did not occur to her; stories that she chose not to tell; and stories which were less well integrated into the account of her life which she presently carries forward. I have not attempted to uncover these less fluid or flattering possibilities. Had she been a public figure, and I been a historian or a biographer, perhaps I would have done so. However, as a researcher involved in a collaborative enquiry with a private citizen, I have not attempted to test or challenge the account that Johanna has offered me. Its value, after all, is as a description of how she understands her experience as a student and a teacher.

Notwithstanding the ethical intention to maintain Johanna's anonymity, I have made no attempt to disguise the broad outline of her story. Disguising certain details – her age, sex, race, country of birth and teaching experience – would have undermined and confused the analysis. Her story is the story of a child of the 1960s, a woman's story, and the story of a fine-arts specialist. Thus, although her name and school have been altered, and the privacy of her friends and colleagues has been protected, it might be possible for well-informed or inquisitive insiders in her own school board to guess her identity. In this case, Johanna's best protection is her informed consent to the publication of the interpretations we have made together.

JOHANNA'S STORY

I started school in a Catholic school in our neighbourhood. From the family stories about it, I just marched right into school and never looked back. Although it was in some ways a good experience for me – I was a successful student – I can remember some of the teachers being quite cruel. On the first day of school, I can remember being asked to hold a box under a crying kid to catch his tears because he really shouldn't be crying. The nuns weren't big on acknowledging that your feelings might have something to do with your reality. At that time I felt that my job was to be intelligent, helpful and well behaved. It was important to me that I be good at maths because my father had recognized that I had some aptitude there. I can remember in Grade 3 when I couldn't figure out borrowing and subtracting, I hid my tests rather than take them home. I was absolutely terrified. It was not OK for me to be stupid. Finally, I had to tell my father and he said, 'Well this is simple, I'll teach you a way to do this', and

I learned it right away. I continued to be good at school – not the brightest in the class, but I did well. I took my religion seriously, too. In Grade 8, I decided that I wanted to be a nun. I can remember researching it and visiting convents. The nuns were really keen but I don't think my parents had any idea what was going on. When I told my parents that what I wanted was to enter a convent, they said, 'No you won't! You are going to the local public high school.' I can remember crying and crying, but knowing there was no choice. You did what your parents said, so off I went to the public high school.

The first year of high school was a nightmare for me. I was only 13, a year younger than most of the others in Grade 8, and I was much less mature. Some of the other kids were already really caring about the way their socks were rolled. I had spent eight years wearing uniforms and I just *wore* my clothes, that was it. When I got to high school I found that your status depended on exactly what you wore and how you did your hair, how you looked and how you could talk. I was a disaster. I remember all of a sudden looking down and thinking, 'This is not what I should be wearing.' It may only have been a couple of months until I figured out what I had to do to fit in. Once I did sort it out, I promised myself that I would never pick on anybody in the way I had been picked on. High school was just a social event. I did well but I remember very little about the courses I took. It was mostly trying to sort out who I was and what I was interested in. I ended up realizing that I was going to be eccentric. The two friends that I ended up with in high school were both popular but not in the preppy football player crowd, they were seen as a little bit crazy.

I hadn't thought at all about college. I was a real baby I guess. I never thought ahead, just figured that someone would decide it for me. My Dad wanted me to go to a school that had brick walls and ivy growing up them, so the next year I went off to the small college in Pennsylvania with all of the Ivy League trappings. There were very few women, which made it wonderful for dating. I had my first experience of being a desirable 'item', with all the negative connotations that has of being regarded by men as a toy or a possession. But the women tended to be much brighter than the men because the standard of acceptance for the men was lower. A lot of guys came in for the big football team. It was a sorority/fraternity school. Everybody wanted to get into the right fraternity and the right sorority. I knew I didn't want to be part of that group of girls who wore the co-ordinating outfits. I don't know whether it was a reverse snobbism or a fear that I wouldn't actually fit because I wasn't comfortable in those clothes or with those people. Instead, I made friends among the crazies in a Jewish fraternity. They were wonderful, wild people. They had the sixties college boys' approach to women, but somehow it was less phoney and more fun than in the Waspy fraternity houses.

By the time I had done my second year I knew I had to get out of this college. The place was oppressively preppy. I thought, 'This place is full of people not like me and I want to get out of here.' So, I applied to a university in New York City and I got in for my junior year. I don't know where I thought I was going with my education or what the use of it was to me. I had started university as a mathematics major but for most of my electives I had chosen philosophy courses. I was fascinated by knowledge and was trying to figure out life and that seemed to me purpose enough at the time. Although I had no music or art in school, I had taken art courses in my first two years of college and I was really excited because it looked as if I might have some talent and it was fun. I loved doing it, and I liked the artists, they were wonderful people. I spoke to my Dad and said I might major in art and he said, 'No, you won't! You'll major in English because you can always be a teacher.' So, I said OK and I took courses in communications, in TV and in English literature.

At about this time – 1968 – I was awakened politically. All my friends were being drafted or trying to evade the draft some way or other and I began to notice what was happening in the world, where the power was held, what was going on. The university had planned to expand into an area which had tenements in it, to put a gym facility where people were living. The students who were involved in outreach programmes into the community reported to the general mass that the university was about to do this. Many students did not want people thrown out of their homes so that we could have gym facilities, and so there were protests organized. At the same time it became known that the university was investing money in companies that were producing napalm and supporting the war in other ways. Students who were opposed to what the university was doing took over various buildings, led by a very left-wing group called Students for a Democratic Society. I never became a member of it but some of my friends were involved and they moved into the headquarters of the administration. Other students occupied other buildings on campus and I

11

joined one such group. People would be discussing what was going on, giving background information, and talking about what to do when the police came and how to protect yourself. The protest was so successful that classes were abandoned for the rest of the year, and at the graduation everybody wore black armbands. It was heady stuff.

After graduation I wanted to go into educational television so I went up to Boston and had some interviews: the only thing they wanted a woman to do was type. At this time, there was no educational TV in New York but there was a desperate shortage of teachers. I completed nine credits in education in a summer course and, without any practice teaching, was sent to a school in the South Bronx. The Black and Puerto Rican people in the school's neighbourhood were living in projects that had been built by the city. Because of drugs and the other ways that those people were destroyed, the projects were fast becoming really dangerous places. People were sniping off the roofs at white people who were in the neighbourhood. The kids were hungry and they were dirty. It was a mess. So, I went in there and for the first year did supply teaching. It soon became clear that I was good at that kind of thing, that I had a 'natural' authority. Not everyone found it so easy. I got a friend of mine a job supply teaching and remember her having lots of trouble. When she was having trouble with a class I would just pop in and whip them into line. Such bravado. I met a couple of neat teachers in this school, one whose style I just loved. He was very laid back and he just loved the kids. He taught Grade 1. He cuddled them and they loved him. He went to their houses and had dinner with their families. I longed to be as at ease and friendly with the kids. He was part of their real lives. I also met a young guy – Doug – who was very keen and also just out of university. We watched these two teachers who had been there before us team teaching, and we decided we wanted to do something like that the next year.

Doug and I had become friends, and he was going to Russia that summer. He said, 'Why don't you come travelling?' I said, 'I don't want to go to Russia', and he said, 'Fly over with me and see Europe instead.' I had never thought of travelling, but I realized I had the money and a companion for at least part of the trip. I packed my knapsack and off I went. We entertained ourselves on the flight over learning to say, 'I have left my handbag in the washroom', in Russian. My parents didn't say a thing. I must have been fulfilling a family dream. It's amazing when I think of it now: I was totally innocent. I had imagined that when I got to London there were going to be little thatched cottages.

On our first day in London, Doug and I went to the movies. As we were looking through the movie listings in the paper we noticed an article on a progressive British infants' school. We thought this looked fascinating, that this was the kind of thing we wanted to do when we returned to New York. The name of the headmaster and the address of the school – in a working-class area of London – were mentioned in the article. We phoned him up and asked if we could visit him. The school was grand. The kids were everywhere, doing all sorts of exciting things. Basically, the approach was individualized activities for kids. Everybody seemed busy and there was all sorts of work up and around, and the kids were happy. I didn't see anybody being lectured to. It was a very happy family atmosphere.

I had booked a passage from Brindisi to Athens and a plane back from Athens to Amsterdam, and Doug planned to go straight to Russia. The day after he left, I was wandering around in Hyde Park because there was a Rolling Stones concert and I sat down next to a guy and we started talking. We fell passionately in love and moved in with each other from the first day. We did some travelling together – but I never got to Greece.

At the end of the summer I left the guy I had met in the park and returned to New York and to teaching in the South Bronx. Doug and I got our own classes. I had Grade 2 and he had Grade 3 and we decided we'd try to teach the classes together. We read Sylvia Ashton-Warner, we made groups, we used word cards and we tried to teach reading. Basically, because we knew nothing about what we were doing, had never had a course in teaching reading, we invented it. Who knows how our kids did, but we were good-willed! I still remember the kids. There was one little girl, a sweet kid who never had a notebook to bring to class. I thought that I would stop in at her house on the way home and see if I could talk to her Mum and remind her to send a notebook. I knocked on the door and this huge woman answered the door with what seemed to be armloads of children and skirtloads of children around her. I looked at her and at the tiny little hole of a place she was living in. I introduced myself, asked how she was . . . and went away.

One day I had to throw an ex-student of the school out. He was hanging around and they didn't want older kids in the building. After school he followed me as I walked through the projects and up to the elevated subway. He was talking to me, telling me about what he thought of school and how angry he was. Just before the subway train pulled in, he started beating me up. It was weird, the first time I had ever been really attacked by anybody. I didn't know what to do. The subway train pulled up, the doors opened, I stepped in and he stayed out and I just thought, 'What can I do here?' I sat down, did nothing, and went home. I was really shaken and at first I was indignant. I thought, 'Here I am going in trying to help', and then I thought, 'What do you mean? Are you crazy? Nobody asked you to be there, to go there to teach.' So, I stopped thinking that I was somehow going to be immune because of my goodwill.

A few months later I decided to leave New York and move to London to live with the man I had met the previous summer. In retrospect, I see that it was a good time for me to leave New York City. It took me months in London to realize how paranoid I had become in New York. It was a city of constant violence and not a healthy place for me. In London, I found a job right away working in a nursery school in South Kensington, where upper-class people sent their two- to four-year-olds. I think that they were horrified by the thought that an American would be teaching their children. Also, I started teaching kids how to read and there were reports back that I was spelling 'Mummy' the wrong way. I was terribly over-qualified for what I was doing – I was making £13 a week. Although I had great fun with the other teachers, who were all Montessori-trained, I hated the school and the tyrant who ran it. I can remember being absolutely horrified to watch her teach an art class where all the kids sat down and she said, 'Now this is how you draw the train. Make a box. Draw a circle.' So, with complete glee I told her that I had gotten a job making $5,000 a year working at a private American school teaching art. Before I applied for that job I had not thought of teaching art, but I knew that I had to get a decent job. The only preparation I had was a couple of art courses at university, but the head of the department liked me and he felt that I could do it.

The school was huge, with 2,000 children aged from 5 to 18 years. I taught art in the middle school. The teachers were a mixed group, full of energy, many of them there for a two-year stint in London before moving on. I made one crazy friend who had a tremendous influence on me. What a wonderful teacher he was! He had been with the school for years. On the first day of every year he would organize an event for his students. One year he moved an antique wrought-iron bed into his classroom which he festooned with flowers. His students arrived to find him sleeping in the bed wearing a donkey's head. He was teaching *A Midsummer Night's Dream* that year. His walls were covered with newspaper clippings of articles he thought his students should read. When the flowers on his desk died he composed a poem which he put next to them. He was magical. When my daughter, his namesake, was born he wrote to her, 'I hope that you find the world as beautifully outrageous as I am still finding it.'

The school was a weird composite of rich, conservative American parents and many left-wing teachers. My political leanings have always been socialist. One of my friends who taught history at the school was very concerned about the right-wing policies of the then Minister of Education, Margaret Thatcher. He had taken his kids down to see schools in the East End where Margaret Thatcher had just stopped having milk provided free. She had been nicknamed by the British press 'Margaret Thatcher, milk snatcher!' His students were horrified to see the poverty in these neighbourhoods and the idea that this Minister of Education would stop school milk for these kids seemed outrageous to them. There was a genuine anti-Thatcher feeling around the place and it was a shock to hear that she was going to give the speech to dedicate the opening of the new school building. The most concerned students decided that they were going to make a statement. My friend wasn't going to stand in the way of free speech, so the kids stood up and made their speech and walked out of the assembly.

The headmaster felt that it was necessary to expel the students involved and find out which teachers had supported them. It became a huge kerfuffle. The teachers began meeting, divided into opposing camps and the school was in turmoil. Eventually the assistant headmaster lost his job because of his stand on the incident. A dear friend of mine lost her job, and a lot of other teachers left the school. At the very end of it I was summoned to a meeting in the headmaster's office. There were four large men from the embassy, dressed in business suits. One was the cultural attaché who, it was whispered, was from the CIA. Lord knows what kind of anti-American insurrection they imagined was happening. They all wanted to know if I felt there was anything seriously wrong with the school. 'What did I want to change? What

15

would I do differently? Did I think there was a lot of unrest here?' I assured them that I thought everything was fine: who was I to take on the CIA?

I worked there another year after that and then we began thinking of leaving London. I had been looking at England and thinking, 'This country is not built for lasting through the next couple of decades, it hasn't got enough water, it hasn't got enough land, the people are poor, the economy is collapsing. I don't think I want to be here.' History and Mrs Thatcher seem to have proven me wrong. I didn't want to go back to New York, where I would have to worry about people trying to kill me all of the time, so my husband and I decided that Canada might be a sort of middle ground.

We came to Toronto, never thinking that it might be difficult to get a job. I found that I needed more teacher training so I applied to go to the teachers' college. The next year, I got a job teaching a Grade 5 class. I had read some Adler, and done a course in Adlerian psychology and thought I would try that with kids. I went into this Grade 5 in an inner-city school and tried to be Adlerian. It was a disaster! The principal shook his head and said, 'We don't discuss things rationally with these children when they are throwing their desks around.' Anyway, I held on for a year and then he put me in a Grade 3 because he figured that I could handle that better. By that time I had thought, 'Well an Adlerian approach may be good philosophically, but I can't make it work in the classroom.' So I went back to my old teaching style which had always worked.

Towards the end of the year I discovered that I was probably going to get the sack because of declining enrolment. I realized that if I got more qualifications I could get a job that was more secure, so that summer I took two music courses. It was the first music education I had had since I had taken piano lessons as a kid. That summer was a marathon, but I learned to play just about every instrument in the orchestra. Early in 1978, a job came up teaching music in a school where the principal was having problems with his music programme. I considered his job offer, and thought, 'Nah! I don't want to do this. I don't know anything about music. I can play Hot Cross Buns on the tuba, but who cares!' The principal took me to see several classes and we ended up in Miles and Bob's room.

[These two teachers were eventually to become her colleagues at Community School.]

They convinced me to take the job. When I walked into their room there were kids everywhere. They were under the tables, they were on top, they had built partitions, they were doing a newspaper, but they were all working. Miles looked me right in the eye and said, 'You really want to come here, this'll be a great place for you.' So I said OK, and I took the job teaching Grade 7 and 8 music.

The principal of the school – call it Prince Albert School – was pleased to have me teach his music programme. I think he was impressed by the fact that I had survived teaching in the South Bronx, and he told me what he really needed was 'a wrestler who could hum'. In the beginning, I found that teaching music was really stressful. I had fourteen different classes, seven Grade 7s and seven Grade 8s. First of all I had to teach myself how to teach music without a tremendous amount of musical skill. It gave me the advantage of knowing where most of the kids were, and I felt that was important. The fact that I could understand how little they knew made me a different kind of music teacher than any they had had before. Someone who was a fine musician might have a hard time getting back to the real beginnings of any kind of musical knowledge. Anyhow, this is how I reasoned with myself about my lack of musical knowledge. I had learned to play guitar in university and figured that I could use that in my teaching so I collected about 30 guitars, and taught the kids to play and sing along.

The first year I was at Prince Albert School, Miles and Bob asked me to do the music for the show they were putting on, *Bugsy Malone*. I hadn't a clue what to do so I asked which kids could play, and we collected a group of kids who could play saxophone, bass and piano. With the help of the itinerant music teachers we created a little jazz group for the play's nightclub act. I taught the rest of the kids to sing the songs using the record. They loved it and the musical was fun, but it brought up the whole antagonism between what Miles and Bob were doing and the rest of the school. When they did a play what became important was the play and so when they had to stop their kids from going to classes for two days in order to do the dress rehearsals the rest of the staff, who were already quite antagonistic towards them, became even angrier. Of course, everybody loved the play when it happened, but it created a bad feeling among the rest of the staff, as it seems it will in any school – even Community School.

During this time I also did all kinds of experimental music. One year a friend who was a composer came in and composed music with the kids. I did dance and music and a lot of creative things. When you have that much time to fill with music, you really have to figure out what you are going to do, especially if you are not adept at teaching minor scales! When the art teacher at the school decided to leave, I volunteered to switch to art. Because of declining enrolments, the position became half-time art and music. I got to do the art which I loved, and did much less music. I also became interested in teaching drama. I fell into the habit of doing Christmas shows which combined art, music, dance and drama. They became increasingly adventurous, leading up to one mammoth undertaking on the battle between light and dark. The play which held the show together involved three children's journey through the underworld, accompanied by a Chinese dragon who had defected during a tour with the Chinese Opera and was now looking for St George. The basic structure of the play was created by a group of us: a playwright, two puppeteers, my art consultant and me. It was a silly and talented group and the play was quite marvellous. We had 15 different puppet shows happening as you came into the building. One class did a little nativity play, and others did a shadow play, or sang songs, or danced to a snowflake poem.

When I think about it, it was just astounding. I probably had more fun than anybody else in the doing of it, but there were two problems. One was the perennial problem of staff who were concerned about disruption caused by the performance. The other problem was that I felt that the play was too much mine: the kids were following plans made by others, and being told what to do and how to feel. I realized that this was not what I wanted for these kids. I wanted to give them access to the beauty in their lives, I wanted to teach them to see and hear but their pubescent minds were spinning with much bigger issues: 'Who am I? Do I look OK? How can I make people like me? Can I afford to disagree? Will there be a world left for me to grow up in?' And mostly, 'Don't bore me. I know there's exciting stuff out there.'

I am not sure why, it may just have been expedient, but about this time I went on to do an additional qualification course in drama. This course changed my whole approach to drama and what I thought could be accomplished by using drama in teaching. I had the experience of 'going into role', which is something I had never had in all my life. It was so exciting to see the potential for being in someone else's shoes as a learning experience. I started doing drama this way with the kids and I found that I could do it. It was exhausting, though, because it is such a scary thing for kids. Kids get to hide themselves in a lot of other classes, and they can't in drama. The level of their ability to jump into the drama makes the drama good or bad, so if you can't structure the drama so that they are actually willing to make that leap and join you in this role-playing then you've lost them and the experience is awful for everybody. Now, because I understood going into role, I had a lot of sympathy for kids who just could not see any sense in it. I spent a lot of time trying to create warm-up activities that would get them ready to join in, and giving them situations that they were able to connect with.

The next year we did a final Christmas show and a play at Prince Albert, but I had burnt out with the rest of the staff. I never managed to put on a play without annoying the rest of the staff. If I had managed to do it all in my own time I might have been more popular, but I figured they were not liking me for doing the shows and I didn't want to be in that position any more.

That was when I got the second invitation to join Bob, Freida and Miles, who by now had started Community School. I really thought long and hard about it. After I visited the school I was not at all sure that I could work in that atmosphere, but it seemed to me that I was between a rock and a hard place. I was ready to change schools and Community School was the best offer available. In the beginning of the year at Community School, when they started planning for the camping trip, I was really impressed. The atmosphere of the place was so different from any place I had taught in before. The kids were not the enemy, we were a group, a family to take care of each other. That in itself was revolutionary. I was high on that feeling, it was wonderful. The kids were doing things that made sense. They were learning processes of organization and taking charge, and it seemed wonderful to me. The kids were very happy.

I was going to be teaching the art, music and drama, and I thought that was all that would be required of me. And then the weight of what you do have to do at Community School began to appear. We would spend every Thursday afternoon trying to schedule for the next week. There was no outline timetable, and the lack of routines that made life difficult for the kids. It was very hard to teach because the kids wouldn't show up on time. In addition, I was a new person in the school and the kids were out to prove that I was going to be someone awful. Many Grade 8s were unbelievably rude and obnoxious and nasty, but

19

by the end of the year I had won over most of the kids. The others, who were so involved in their own worlds that they had no room for teachers, just tolerated me.

When things go well at Community School, they go very well. One example is a drama class from last year where we were dealing with situations of peer pressure. We did some warm-up and some game-play before the class, just to get them feeling comfortable moving around the class and talking to each other. Then I described the scenario that they had to act out. They were in groups of three or four and one or two people in the group were being pressured by the other two to do something they really didn't feel comfortable with. Perhaps they were going to a party where they knew there would be drinking, or drugs. The kids really got involved in what they were doing. I could hear conversations that I have heard around the school, and I watched some of them trying to deal with the pressure as I went from group to group. I thought that it would be a good idea to have them look at what was happening in each of the groups, so the kids did their scene for the rest of the groups. For me, it was a tremendous learning experience because I was able to focus the kids on particular questions. Why did this person give in, why did that person? What kinds of arguments is that person using? There was a wonderful group, where two of the really together, cool kids – the ones who were respected for being really on top of things – acted the parts of the kids who didn't want to get involved in the drugs or drink. They both dealt with the pressure in very different ways, but one of the ways was simply to remove themselves and yet maintain their dignity. It was such a thing to watch, to see that happen. I thought that this was incredible modelling for the rest of these kids who feel that they have to somehow placate the people who want them to do things they are not comfortable with.

The reason that the class seemed such a wonderful class to me was that the issue of learning to say 'No', being able to think independently, having the words to get yourself out of a bad situation, seems to me such an important skill in life. It is essential for your own mental health and self-protection to be able to get out of a bad situation. The kids really seemed to have learned something. As they left they said, 'Let's do that again, that was really interesting, I want to do more of this kind of thing.'

Teaching provides me with a way of developing my interests in philosophy and psychology and the arts. My teaching has all been wrapped up in a search for who I am and the meaning of my own life, as pretentious as that might sound, and with my desire to enrich the lives of others. What I have done is replace religion with psychological health and fulfillment and the ability to have joy in my life. Seeing ways to approach that in my own life shows me that I can do that with kids. I can show them ways to deal with things that will make them, to my mind, psychologically healthy and able to see the joy that is there and to deal with the bad stuff as well.

Right now I have the freedom to really do what I want to do with the kids, which is an unbelievable freedom. Very, very few teachers have the freedom I have to work with people I know and love, and do what I want to do without having too much interference from people who are trying to tell me what I ought to be doing. I will be in a wonderful situation at Community School, provided I can find ways to make it less exhausting. If I were to go on to do something else, I don't see myself wanting to get away from kids. I would not, for instance, try to get a job as an art consultant because the kind of work that I would be required to do would not interest me. Perhaps I could change the job in the same way that I have changed other things to make them into what I want to do, but at the moment I don't see myself going out looking for anything else. I haven't found out what I can do with Community School and can see myself being there for years and years before I need to do anything else.

HOPES AND DREAMS

Behind this story lie the hopes and dreams which shape the unfolding story of Johanna's life. The quality of her relationships is the touchstone of Johanna's personal and professional life. When she talks about schools and teachers she admires, she talks in terms of the warmth of the relationships between staff and students. She presumes that there is a direct connection between students' emotional state and their learning, so she acknowledges the students' feelings in her classroom teaching and accepts responsibility for supporting students who are finding their relationships at home or school difficult. Not only does she work to make close friendships at school, but also she brings into her classroom the people who are important in her own private life. As visitors, volunteers or as artists in residence, a series of close friends have been involved in Community School in the time I have known her.

21

Johanna believes that arts are essential to the mental health of a community. Her appreciation of the arts is not the dry as dust judgement of a critic, but the practical appreciation of a participant. When she teaches music, she places a higher value on introducing everyone to the guitar than on improving the skills of accomplished musicians. The latter group, she figures, already know the pleasure of music-making and will pursue their interests in their own time. Similarly, her teaching of art and drama emphasizes participation by all rather than technical excellence of the most able. In Johanna's classes, professional artists are not the unknown and unapproachable experts who may be admired in galleries or in performance, but friends and acquaintances who drop in and share their skills and enthusiasm with her students.

All of her life Johanna has felt that it was important to try hard to do well, a trait she connects with her parents' high expectations for her as a child. As a teacher, this is evident in her solid preparation for classes, the bright and cheerful displays in her room and her willingness to take on additional tasks. Johanna is a hard-working, energetic teacher, a person who has always organized school plays, concerts and excursions. The dark side of this quality, however, is that she often feels very critical of the quality of her work. If only she worked harder or knew more, she sometimes feels, she could make a difference to the lives of the students she has failed to touch.

Unlike many teachers, Johanna did not have discipline and management problems when she began teaching. It was this experience, not how well she could teach minor scales, which recommended her to the principal who first employed her to teach music. She provides a happy, busy, purposeful classroom atmosphere in her art and music classes, where individual students' needs and intentions may be honoured. She admires the kind of child-centred work which characterizes Community School on a good day, but feels nervous when students do not seem to know what they should be doing. On this issue there are significant differences of opinion between the three staff at Community School. More than the other teachers, she believes that there needs to be a structure which supports students' independent learning. The problem of just how much structure there should be and how it should be organized continued to concern Johanna throughout the life of the study.

In some ways, Johanna may be thought to be a very conventional person. She was good at school, attended two expensive private colleges, and has spent nearly 20 years working in a job that is (in Canada, at least) respected and well paid. She has taken additional qualification courses which allow her to reach the top of the salary scale for classroom teachers. She values the safety and long-term security of her employment and she expects to teach for another 20 years before she retires to enjoy the benefits of her superannuation scheme. At a personal level, however, Johanna is much less conventional. She has made a series of bold changes in direction, sometimes in order to be employed and at other times following her heart or changes in her personal interests. She has taught in three countries, in slum schools and élite schools, in conventional schools and alternative schools. Wherever she has been, she has maintained a separation from the mainstream: from children who would turn their socks just so; from young women in twin sets and pearls who dated football players; and from teachers who had a narrow academic focus. As a teacher, she has identified with the rabble-rousers, not those who impose things from above. For ten years she has taught subjects many of her colleagues regard as marginal, and for much of that time she has acted as broker between her schools and a group of people teachers regard as even more marginal, the artists who work in schools on short-term Arts Council grants.

Chapter 2

Repertoire

This chapter consists of six stories about Johanna's teaching during autumn 1988. The particular stories I have chosen to tell in this chapter are of lessons which come from Johanna's repertoire. By her repertoire, I mean those lessons which have been rehearsed and refined over the years and which form the experiential basis for the new lessons she invents each day. The first group of stories illustrates some of the ways she teaches art, in 'Fishes' and 'Fastwurms', and music, in 'Fingers Like Hammers' and 'Pictures with Music'. The second set of stories describes some of the ways in which she helps students to learn from their experiences, in 'Camping' and 'Conferences'. Considered together, these stories provide a concrete introduction to the way in which Johanna's hopes and dreams for education are expressed when she is dealing with familiar territory. These are examples of the kinds of lessons that work without planning, the ones Johanna knows she can make up as she goes along.

Before proceeding with the stories, a brief comment about my narrative voice. Most often, I am a minor actor in the stories, a person who was there at the time and who is telling the stories as they unfolded to me. Less often, I am an omniscient narrator who explicitly interprets the story for readers with the benefit of information not available to the more naïve 'I' who inhabits the stories. I do not know everything about these characters' actions and intentions, but I do have the benefit of working with the stories over an extended time. Consequently, the stories carry two different kinds of interpretation. First, there are the interpretations I made at the time, the events I chose to include in my field records and the conclusions I drew about them as I sat and wrote at the end of each day. Second, there are interpretations which result from the process of selecting, editing and rewriting the field notes into this set of stories. At this stage, I have added a series of introductions, connecting statements and concluding remarks which shape the individual stories as part of the larger story I want to tell about Johanna's teaching and about my own understanding of continuity and change in teachers' knowledge. In order to avoid the possibility that readers may confuse interpretations I made at the time with conclusions I can only draw later in the hermeneutical process, I have adopted several typographical conventions. Each story has a name which appears in the heading at the beginning of the story. A reference to the date the events took place appears in the first few lines of each story. My after-the-fact interpretive remarks are separated from each story by a row of asterisks, or appear in the final section of each chapter, 'Summary and Conclusions'.

And finally, before I turn to the stories, a reminder about where this chapter fits into the larger argument of the study. This chapter contributes a basic building block to the resolution of the substantive problem of enquiry of the study – an attempt to understand how teachers' knowledge changes over time. This chapter describes Johanna's teaching when it is proceeding smoothly, when it is consistent with the biographical imperatives she brings to her work, and when she is in full command of the subject content. Succeeding chapters will explore the ways in which the patterns of her teaching are disturbed by unfamiliar subject content, the processes of reflection she follows as she tries to accommodate to the demands of new contexts for teaching, and the constraints within which her knowledge changes.

ART

Johanna has been teaching art to adolescents for nearly 20 years. This breadth of experience is represented by the two stories which follow. The first, 'Fishes', is a practical art lesson which begins with a brief formal exposition. The second, 'Fastwurms', is a class discussion which followed a gallery visit.

Fishes

Group 1's second formal art lesson of the year (on 14 September) related to the group bulletin-board displays of the material collected on a scavenger hunt of the local farmers' market. Johanna had been pleased with the content of the group work but, as an art teacher, could see some room for teaching more about display graphics. The class of 18 Grade 7 students was seated behind the art tables which were arranged in a U-shape around the blue oriental rug in the centre of the room. Johanna called the roll and then she collected money for some sketchbooks she had offered to buy on behalf of the students. Next, she explained her rules about access to art supplies. Most of the supplies she had were available for student use. Crayons, scissors, clips, pencils and so on were kept in a set of about 20 colourful plastic drawers at the front of the room, and arranged in alphabetical order. Supplies of the most common of these items were also kept near the sink in the hallway in the open-area classroom, so that it would not be necessary for students to come from other classes to borrow supplies from the art room. Paper was available from the open shelves on the south side of the room. Some particularly expensive supplies were kept in the locked cupboards above the sink on the north side of the room. There were also some supplies kept among Johanna's private things in her desk. The desk was not locked, and Johanna asked students not to look through her desk things without permission. There was also a recycling box for scraps of coloured paper, kept near the bin.

Johanna began the lesson proper by explaining that they were going to 'talk a little bit of art talk today'. She drew attention to the set of six black-and-white designs which she had clipped to the top rail of the blackboard. She reminded people of the ideas of 'balance' and 'negative space', which had been introduced in the previous art lesson, and asked whether there was one design that anyone preferred. Most students seemed to have a favourite. Johanna asked several of them to nominate the one they preferred and to say what it was that they liked about it. One student liked the firm straight lines across the bottom of a design which reminded him of a streetscape. Another liked a diagonal design, which was balanced, had some interesting negative spaces and avoided clear horizontals and verticals. As Johanna went around the circle asking for opinions, the whole group was very focused on the task.

Johanna then wrote 'The elements of art' on the blackboard and asked the class to suggest elements that they had learned about last time. They offered 'positive space', 'negative space' and 'balance'. To these she added 'value'. She went on to say that the idea of value was tricky but she would give some examples. She chose a black and a white piece of paper and explained that these were at opposite ends of the value scale:

> This is as light as you can get and this is as dark
> as you can get. So, values are the lights and darks.
> Now if you've got a black and white picture it's very
> easy to tell the value of everything because you have
> black, greys and white and it is easy to tell which is
> the lighter and darker grey. So you have very clear
> values in your picture. But when you start using colour
> it is really hard to tell which is the lightest and which
> is the darkest.[1]

(14 September, p. 177)

While she talked the students listened in silence, some looking down at their desks or books, several drawing or scribbling on their file covers. When Johanna picked up a collection of coloured paper fish from the desk, and asked for a volunteer to come out and arrange the fish from light to dark the atmosphere of the room changed suddenly. The students were very interested in participating and watched closely as a volunteer began to sort the fish and place them in a line on the rug in the centre of the floor. Johanna said that she found it helpful to squint her eyes when she was trying to compare values because this way, 'the shapes sort of disappear into one another'. When the first girl finished Johanna said, 'Very, very close. Is there anybody who feels that there should be a change?' Johanna chose one of several volunteers and asked him to make the changes he saw, and agreed that the fish were now sorted from the lowest to the highest value.

Next Johanna explained that values were important in art because they provided contrast:

> The reason I thought we might look at values is
> because your bulletin boards, which you are working
> on now, are going to be more effective if you have

good contrast. So, I would like you to look at
how things change depending on what we put
behind it. If we put something close in value,
say if I put this behind this fish, look what
the fish does. Now, if I take something further
away in value look what it does, it shows up
better.

(14 September, p. 178)

Johanna went on to give several more examples of fish against
backgrounds to illustrate this point and then demonstrated a series
of other ideas for the bulletin boards – using borders, cutting out
shapes to put behind a fish, using arrows to draw attention to a
shape.

After this presentation, Johanna asked students to continue
working on their bulletin-board displays, using the ideas they
had just been talking about. Students began moving around
the room finding their partners and choosing the art supplies
they would need. Some of them went into the open area to look
at their displays. Johanna and I walked around the art room,
helped students find materials and talked to them about their
displays.

This lesson was repeated, after the morning break, with Group
3, a class of 28 Grade 8 students. Unlike the Grade 7 class, this group
was quite restless. Perhaps ten of them arrived late and had to record
their lateness on the blackboard. When the fish-sorting activity
started, there was not the same enthusiasm for the task. Johanna had
to ask people to watch and be silent in order to allow the student who
was sorting the fish to concentrate. Several more times she called
them back to order. In each case they responded, but their attention
to the task did not last long. They were attentive, without being
reminded, at times when Johanna was making a formal explanation
or when a student was doing a demonstration. Their level of attention
seemed to depend on the entertainment value of the activity. If it
was interesting or clearly focused, they did not need reminding.
The class – Johanna included – always seemed poised on the edge of
the the possibility of a joke. At one point Geoffrey was making
little monster noises to himself. Johanna noticed and said that the

monsters were always her favourites on *Sesame Street*, a comment which led to a series of noises and faces representing people's favourites from *Sesame Street*. She apologized, saying that she had done just what she asked them not to do, create a diversion to the lesson which was taking place. A few minutes later, when Johanna was demonstrating how a graphic arrow draws attention to whatever it points to, she held the paper arrow up against the head of a likeable and popular boy. Predictably this led to one student repeating 'What', drawing attention to the fact that Johanna had called George a *What*ever not a *Who*ever, and another person calling out 'Geek', naming the 'What'.

At the end of the demonstration part of the lesson, Johanna was firmer than she had been with the Grade 7 class about the possibility of moving out into the big room to work on the displays. They were to work on the displays, but only in the art room. As the students began to collect their supplies and talk to their group members about their displays, Johanna and I answered a series of questions about art supplies. She stopped several students who planned to leave the room for one reason or other, and then we moved around the class talking to students about their artwork. At one point, Johanna noticed that Mark was sitting reading a book. She sat down next to him and asked him what he was doing. This conversation was part of a continuing dialogue between Johanna and Mark about participation in group work. Mark is very keen to lead activities, but does not like it when people are not so eager to follow. Consequently, he often prefers to withdraw from class activities. Johanna talked to him for some time and then drew in Guy, a lively and popular boy, who was sitting at the same table and was in the same group for this activity. Soon, Mark was off looking for some coloured paper and cutting out fish to go with his group's display.

* * *

In 'Fishes', Johanna is pursuing a series of goals simultaneously. In addition to the art content of the lesson, she is establishing rules and routines for the rest of the year's art lessons, she is continuing from last year her work with Mark's difficulties in being included in group activities, and she is providing some theoretical and practical assistance on a school activity which originated outside her classroom.

The idea for the sequence of lessons on graphic design came from the community life of the school. Originally, in the first week of the school year, the teachers had organized the scavenger hunt to help students from the three classes to mix together so that the Grade 7s were more quickly integrated into the school community. Beyond that, they had decided one lunch time that some pin-up board displays would be a good way for students to communicate what they had learned about the farmers' market. In turn, this led Johanna to decide to do some direct teaching about graphics to help them get more from the activity. The plans of the lessons themselves – the coloured cut-out fish and the group of stools gathered intimately around the rug in the centre of the floor – are part of the established repertoire of art lessons Johanna carries forward from year to year.

Johanna normally offers the same art and music lessons to all three of her classes. The activities and teaching points remain the same, but the details of the lessons vary. Some of these variations are unpredictable and accidental, according to the moods, interests and intentions of particular students in each class. Other variations seem to be more consistent. Group 1 and 2, the two Grade 7 classes, are quite similar. They are both cheerful, interested and biddable, and Group 2 seems a little more lively than Group 1. From the very first lessons of the year, however, the Grade 8 class (Group 3) was less predictable and always more difficult to manage. Part of the difference may be explained by the difference in class size – 26 students rather than 18 or 19 – but part also relates to the history of the school. The previous year, when these students were in Grade 7, they were often able to arrive late for class without penalty and able to move in and out of the room during lessons. It was these patterns of behaviour that led Johanna to move her lessons from the open area to her present self-contained classroom. The class size, the students' history, and the Grade 8s' sense that they were now the senior students in the school meant that Johanna had some difficulty convincing students to be as co-operative as the Grade 7s seemed naturally to be. In this lesson the difficulty was expressed in their lateness, and Johanna's response was to institute a set of penalties for lateness, which she continued to enforce rigorously for the remainder of the term, and in modifying the lesson plan so that the Grade 8s stayed in the art room whereas the Grade 7s had previously been allowed to move out into the open area to work on their displays.

The Grade 8 lesson also exemplifies the careful balancing act Johanna sets for herself in teaching. She uses her lively sense of humour to gather in wayward students and to lighten the mood of the classroom, but continually runs the risk that her jokes will dissolve the delicately balanced working environment of the lesson. In the second lesson in 'Fishes', she chose to make a lighthearted comment about Geoffrey, who had drifted off into the world of *Sesame Street*. A little later, having already apologized for creating the monster diversion, she pointed the arrow at George's head and brought on another round of diversions. Her classes, consequently, are fun to be in but require considerable reserves of energy to manage, especially with the less tractable Grade 8 students in Group 3.

Fastwurms

During the second full week of school, Johanna arranged to take her classes to the Art Gallery of Ontario (AGO) to see an exhibition by a group of three Toronto artists who call themselves Fastwurms. The exhibition included some site-specific constructions, created in and for the gallery, and some pieces which had previously been exhibited. The site-specific pieces included a large and mysterious raft assembled from polythene pipes and tarpaulin, resting on crates of canned food, fruit juice and beer. A light shone through the tent and past the copper oak leaves of a bush chandelier, casting eerie shadows on the gallery wall behind. A tape loop softly played the sound of the three Fastwurms dancing in the gallery as they made the raft. Other pieces included a deck of huge acrylic cards, each telling stories related to organs of the body, and a set of rattles, head-dresses and altarpieces made from birch bark, feathers and copper wire. The exhibition was complex and challenging, playfully running together textures and images from the bush with synthetic fabrics and high-gloss acrylic surfaces.

31

All three groups were interested and serious visitors to the gallery. Like me, they didn't quite know what to make of it, but they willingly sat and sketched objects that they liked.

Following the gallery visit, Johanna talked with her classes about their reactions to Fastwurms. In these lessons, she had each class sit on their art stools in a circle around the rug in the centre of the art room. The Group 1 discussion (21 September) began with Johanna asking students about their reactions. One student thought that it was 'pretty neat but very strange' because the artists had changed the size, texture or materials of familiar objects. Another student commented that the oversize playing cards were strange because paintings were usually flat.

> *Elise*   There was one painting of the birch bark dog that had green grass hanging out, all of these things hanging off.
>
> *Johanna* Paintings are usually flat?
>
> *Elise*   Yes.
>
> *Johanna* When you go to the museum you generally don't expect to find things popping out of the painting? So this was a change for you. They seem to feel that paintings can come out from the surface. Other artists have done that too. Who else had a comment? Who hasn't made a comment? Frances.
>
> *Frances* I didn't like any of it.
>
> (21 September, p. 204)

Not only did Frances not like the work, she thought that it did not belong in a formal gallery such as the AGO. As the discussion developed, several students expressed reservations about the quality of what they had seen:

> *Peter*   I'd agree with Frances on that because there are some really brilliant artists who just

paint what is there in the world and you can
tell what it is.

Johanna   It's hard to know what is good when you really
            can't see the skill involved, is that what you're
            saying? It's hard to know whether it's worth
            millions or is just a square on a paper, and
            maybe they are just trying to trick us. . . . It's
            hard to put your finger on what's a good artist.
            Mira?

Mira   A good artist is someone who paints what they
            like, but if they paint what they like a good
            artist - what most people would say is a good
            aritst - is someone who paints things that other
            people like. If I didn't like that art show I
            would say that those artists weren't very good
            artists, that I didn't enjoy what they had
            painted.

Johanna   So, what the person who sees it *likes* has a
            great deal to do with whether or not they think
            the artist is any good.

            (21 September, p. 205)

As students made their contributions to the discussion, Johanna
repeated what she thought they had said, sought clarification if necessary, and moved on to another of the many students waiting patiently
for an opportunity to speak.

Johanna   Betsy?

Betsy   Say the artist has something in mind and they
            paint it, well when other people see it they
            might not see the same thing.

Johanna   Umm, that's a complicated thought! The
            painting might have a different meaning for the
            artist than it has for the viewer. [*Writes on
            board*:] 'The painting could have lots of different
            meanings.'

Johanna   Elise, and then Frances.

Elise   I think that what Jeremy said about the artist mostly thinking about themselves, his feeling when he paints the picture, most artists draw one picture that's how *they* feel. Say I'm Picasso and I draw a picture of my feelings and then I draw a picture that other people would like, a certain age group, maybe that senior citizens would like it or something.

Johanna   Let me see if I have got you, if I understand you. You're saying that artists paint differently depending on who their audience is. [*Writes on board*:] 'Artists paint differently depending on who their audience is.'

Elise   Yeah.

Johanna   Frances?

Frances   There are really a lot of fashions. You can't just say, 'This is really great art', and [therefore] it is, and then say, 'You don't have any taste because you don't like it.' We don't all have the same taste. This person might see a modern artist like Picasso and really like it and that person might say, 'Oh, I don't really like it as much as you.' You can't just say it's no good just because you don't like it.

Johanna   So, to criticize someone for their artistic taste, when really what they are talking about is just what they prefer, not what's good or not . . .

Frances   . . . because the artist might appeal only to a certain group of people. Some people might like to go to modern art and others might not.

(21 September, pp. 206–7)

Notwithstanding Frances' pluralism, many students continued to be sceptical about the value of modern art. Were such artists too poor at drawing to represent objects accurately, or were they just too lazy? Another student, Thalia, defended non-representational art by describing her experience of visiting a gallery in Washington DC:

Thalia   We went to the Fishorn Museum and it was all modern art and I liked it so much because it was all so different and very interesting. I agree with Penny because modern art, I think that modern art is there to show that things can be done in different ways. It doesn't have to be the same tradition. Because the traditional way shows what I can see all the time. But modern art doesn't.

Johanna   OK. Thalia just made a very interesting suggestion. She said that what a traditional painting shows is something you can see all of the time with your eyes anyway and a modern painting shows you something new. And that's a very important thing when we are talking about art that artists and art critics talk about artists needing to do. They say that artists need to show us the world differently than we would ever see it. That is a way of looking at art. It's just one way, it might not be the way you choose. But they say that [*She writes on the board*:] 'Artists show us something new about the world.' If we use this rule for art, how would we judge the Fastwurms exhibit? Were they showing us anything new? Frances.

Frances   They were, but they got a bit too carried away. They tried to make it interesting but they went too far, it was so ugly. They went too far.

(21 September, p. 209)

When Frances called Fastwurms' work 'ugly', Johanna went to the blackboard and drew a line on the board, placing herself at one end and Frances at the other. She said that the rest of the class would need to think about where they would put themselves on the line. When Martina spoke Johanna placed her on the line she had drawn on the board. Next, Johanna mentioned that not everyone had spoken and asked Fletcher what he felt about the exhibition. When he explained his view, Johanna placed him on the line. Then she went around the whole class asking everyone to nominate where they fitted on the line she had drawn. At the end there was a long line across the board with letters signifying the initial of each student arrayed across it from the extreme of 'loved it' to 'hated it'. There were nearly twice as many on the 'loved it' side than the 'hated it' side of the continuum, with only one student so extreme as to agree with Johanna.

As the lesson drew to a close, Johanna asked people whether they had thought of any questions to ask the artists when they met them at the gallery on 6 October. She asked people to spend the next few minutes writing out questions which she would later collect and pass on to the artist. Those who did not finish could do so for homework. The lesson ended, as every one of Johanna's lessons does, with her routine for dismissing students. Johanna asked table captains to dismiss their group when the area was clean and tidy, and she stood at the door asking each student to name the table captain who had dismissed them before she allowed them to leave the room.

* * *

In this two stories we see how closely Johanna's social and cognitive goals for schooling run together. In 'Fishes', Johanna used the rug as a theatrical space where students sorted brightly coloured fishes while their classmates looked on. In 'Fastwurms', she grouped the class intimately in a circle around the edge of the rug, ensuring that everyone was physically included in the spirited discussion which took place. The content of the discussion addresses an important issue – How can we judge the quality of non-representational art? – but Johanna's communication patterns in the lesson are teaching a second, simultaneous lesson. Her 'repeat and reply' pattern models a way of talking and listening to people which aims to ensure that students know that she has heard and understood what they have said. She does not give the impression that the students' task in the discussion is to guess some correct answer which is already in the teacher's mind. In her discussion with Frances, for example, Johanna demonstrates that she understands what Frances thinks by repeating it back to her and shows that Frances' view is equal to but different from hers by placing their opinions at opposite ends of the same continuum. The continuum activity was a powerful and spontaneous pedagogical act. It began in Johanna's spontaneous response to Frances' diametric opposition to her own views, grew as a way of including the views of someone who had not spoken, and ended up serving the purpose of showing that there was a range of opinion in the class and that many people liked the exhibition.

In 'Fishes', the idea for the lesson came from the community life of the school and the content came from years of practised art teaching. In 'Fastwurms', the idea for the lesson came from Johanna's own fascination with Fastwurms' exhibition at the AGO. She and a friend had been invited to look in at the gallery during the late stages of construction of the display, and had since been back to see the finished work. Johanna thought that the students might share her enthusiasm, and she asked the school board for some financial assistance to arrange for the students to meet the artists at the gallery. Characteristically, Johanna's art lessons do not come from school board or ministry guidelines. They are probably consistent with the guidelines, and if challenged she could no doubt justify her lessons in terms of the guidelines, but these documents offer her no practical assistance or impediment. Instead, she mixes the conceptual apparatus she already carries with her, activities suggested by school and community events, and established patterns of classroom management to create new and different versions of her art teaching practice each year.

MUSIC

Like Johanna's art teaching, her music teaching is an area of long-established and comfortable specialist skill. In the stories that follow, two facets of Johanna's music teaching repertoire are described. The first lesson, 'Fingers Like Hammers', is one of Johanna's whole-class guitar lessons. The second story, 'Pictures with Music', is a music appreciation lesson which also provides a window on Johanna's drama teaching skills.

Fingers Like Hammers

Johanna began Group 2's third guitar lesson (19 October) as she always does with her guitar allocation routine. She called students' names from the class list, following a rotating order in each lesson, so that each person would get an equal number of early choices over the year. The guitars are of unequal quality, and some students prefer classical or folk guitars. As students collected their guitars and returned to their stools, Johanna carefully arranged students in a circle, stressing that she had to be able to see their hands as they played. When she was satisfied, she handed out the song-sheets. Before they started playing she checked their tuning.

Johanna   Starting with Holly we are going to play the chord E minor, which is also the chord we are going to need to play this song. E minor is played with these two fingers, fingers 1 and 2, OK? [*Demonstrates*] Finger 1 goes on string 5, fret 2. Finger 2 goes down on string 4 in fret 2. Now I know that it is hard to see your fingers. Check that you are in fret 2, on strings 5 and 4. Here's what it should sound like – I hope my guitar is in tune – [*Checks and tunes her own guitar. Other students check their tuning and Johanna notices two other guitars out of tune.*] Anybody else? The reason that I use E minor as a tuning chord is that we play all six strings. OK, I am going to teach you a fun bit now. We are going to go back to the first chord we learned, D. Is there anybody who needs help remembering D? OK, finger 1, string 3, fret 2. Finger 2, string 1, fret 2. Finger 3, string 2, fret 3. So, we'll play five strings, 1, 2 ready to strum? Strum.

Johanna	OK, this song has a really nice beginning and it involves putting your pinkie down in the third fret on string 1, at the same time as playing D. So listen to what I do. I play: D, D, new chord, D. When I say 'new chord' put your pinkie down on string 1.
Amy	This sounds funny.
Johanna	Show me. It sounds funny because you are not pressing down hard enough. Fingers like hammers.

(19 October, p. 316)

They practised several times. At the end of each try, Johanna said 'Good for you', or 'So *good* for people who are just learning to play guitar.' When she spotted a student who was not fingering properly she said, 'Brendan, can you reverse fingers 1 and 2, they are upside down.' After a few runs through she moved on to the second skill to be taught in the lesson.

Johanna	Listen to how the whole thing goes. You are going to impress the pants off anyone who plays guitar.

She played the lick she had just taught, four times. First she played it in the second fret, then the fourth, then the seventh and then again in the second. Impressed, several students called out 'OK' or 'All right' in appreciation.

Johanna	That's what you are going to learn to do. You can do it, believe me. You are not doing anything different, you are just gliding it along in different frets. Easy, eh? Try it in the second fret. [*Plays*] Slide them to the fourth fret, slide them to the seventh fret. Listen to it, it should be like this. [*Plays*] Try that. And now back to

39

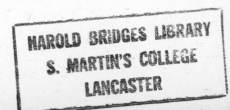
HAROLD BRIDGES LIBRARY
S. MARTIN'S COLLEGE
LANCASTER

the second fret. Ready, and . . . [*Plays*].
Let's practice it again.

(19 October, p. 317)

Having played it through once without instruction, Johanna asked for volunteers who would like to show off. Jack volunteered – something he would never do in an academic subject – played, and finished with a grin of triumph on his face. After each student finished, Johanna said 'Good!' or 'You are almost there' or 'Pretty impressive!' and then went on to explain how the person could improve the sound, by fretting the D in the correct fret or pressing harder ('Fingers like hammers!') or by cutting her nails. Perhaps half of the class played individually and then Johanna decided to have the whole class play together again. She noticed that not everyone could keep up so she said, 'Let's do it again, slower.'

After several practices at increasing speed, the class was ready to look at the song-sheet. Johanna pointed out that there were a few chords that people wouldn't know, but they should ignore those and play the ones they knew. She led the class through the chorus first, singing and calling chord changes.

Johanna	Who's completely lost, can't keep up that speed? Penny, Holly, Natalie. You people are learning at normal speed. The other people in this class are startlingly fast. I don't know why, so you must not think of yourself as being behind. I don't understand why you [other] people are able to do this so well, it usually doesn't happen.
Students	People practice at home.
Johanna	Yes, that's probably it.

After they have been right through it once, a student arrived late, from another class.

Johanna	Shall we see if we can impress Raoul?
Students	Yes.

Johanna   OK, hold on to your pants, Raoul.
             1, 2, 3, 4.

             (19 October, p. 318)

They played through the introduction with the lick Johanna
taught at the beginning of the lesson. In the next stage of the lesson,
Johanna led the class right through the song. She sings strongly and
plays a steel-stringed guitar, so that the sound she makes dominates
the group. Students have the feeling that they are playing the song
long before they could do so unaccompanied. When these students got
to the last verse, which includes several chords most students did not
know, she kept playing as the students dropped out and joined in with
her singing. As they finished their first run-through, students were
beaming with satisfaction and calling out, 'All right!' and 'We did the
whole song!'

Johanna shared their enthusiasm, and feigning disbelief at
their skill kidded them: 'You guys!' She moved on to the last
part of the lesson, a request session. She asked what people would
like to play. Several students wanted to play the same song again,
but they settled on one which had been learned before. She quickly
reminded them of the chords, 'It's just D and G, back and forth.
Four Ds, four Gs, four Ds', and then led them straight through,
singing, playing and calling the chord changes. By now it was
time to finish the lesson, so Johanna had five students at a time
return their guitars to the racks, asked table captains to dismiss
their groups, and stood at the door checking that students had
permission to leave.

* * *

Johanna's guitar lessons follow a well-established pattern. As often
as I have watched her, she begins with her routine for distribut-
ing guitars, hands out a song-sheet, draws students' attention to an
aspect of the song which is particularly interesting – the lick, in the
case above – and then practises the song in several separate pieces.
As students learn the chords, she plays her steel-stringed guitar and
sings above their playing. Sometimes she stops the group playing to
allow individual students to 'show off' their mastery of the new chord

or lick. Then she puts as much of the song together as they can manage and finishes the lesson with a request session. If the class has some expert guitarists, she excuses them from the lesson to practise in the hallway outside.

For each of these established patterns, Johanna can give a series of reasons. Sometimes the reasons come from her practical experience of what works for her, and in other cases the reasons are biographical. The reason behind her habit of allowing skilled guitarists to work outside in the hallway, for example, is that it resolves several practical problems of guitar teaching.

> When some of the students are really advanced I let them leave the room to work on a particular piece, as long as they are willing to come back in at the end of the lesson and play what they were working on. They know that I will ask them to, and I know that they have been using their time. It also gives the other students in the class a sense of where they can go. These students are generally very shy to play in front of each other, but if they know that it will get them out of the room if they will come back and show off, then they will sometimes make that step.
>
> (19 October, pp. 322–3)

The thinking behind Johanna's use of praise, to take another example, has strong biographical roots. For Johanna, the effusive praise she offers – 'this class is so fast' – which seems to apply to every class at the time she says it, is a kind of teaching trick. It's not that she is not genuinely pleased, but that the accuracy of the encouragement is much less important to her than the fact of the encouragement. When we talked about 'Fingers Like Hammers' (19 October) Johanna connected her use of praise to her own experience as an adult music student. When she was learning clarinet during the summer when she qualified as a music teacher, she felt very badly treated by the teacher. She had some trouble early on getting a decent sound out of the instrument and was publicly ridiculed. She has never forgotten and never forgiven the teacher. When I said that I had the same sort of experience – when, aged 10, the teacher made me sing in front of the class so that he could grade my singing, and then wrote '4, E, Very weak voice' on my report card – Johanna said that everyone has such a story. The students in her classes, at least, will not get their musical humiliation story from Community School.

Pictures with Music

Later in the term (2 November), Johanna introduced her classes to a different kind of music lesson. In this case she used her background in drama teaching to introduce students to music appreciation. She taught the lesson to Group 1 first, but by the time Group 2 reached the classroom news of the lesson had seeped out into the hallway. As the class came into the room, Peter wanted to know, 'Do we get to do animal noises, too?'

Johanna asked the class to come into the centre of the room and sit on the floor around the rug. Some sat cross-legged on the vinyl floor of the art room, some squatted, and several lay on the floor. Johanna sat cross-legged on the edge of the rug and explained that today's lesson was music appreciation, not guitar. She spoke very softly, drawing the class in close by the level of her voice:

> In our society we get bombarded by all different types of
> music. We get Muzak, elevator music, some music that
> you get to choose and some you don't ask for. So, a lot of
> the music that you hear, you don't understand. In music
> appreciation we listen to different kinds of music so that
> we understand it better. Even if you never get to like it
> you at least know what the person was trying to do.

(2 November, p. 377)

Johanna went on to explain that the music the class was going to listen to today was written by people who wanted to 'paint a picture with music', what she called 'programme music'. She explained that not all composers had this intention. People like Bach, for example, were not interested in creating pictures in music. Then, she went on to demonstrate what fine distinctions people were able to make between similar sounds. She asked people to close their eyes and then she dropped a quarter, a dime and a penny on the floor. Most of the class thought that they could tell the difference the first time she dropped the coins, but she asked them not to say in what order she dropped the coins. She then dropped them a second time and asked people to say in what order she had dropped them. By then, almost everyone guessed correctly.

Having demonstrated what subtle differences every student could make, Johanna explained that the class was going to do some 'sound compositions' today. First, she talked for a time about some of the ways people can make sounds without musical instruments:

> There are lots of different types of claps. I once did a
> piece of music with some people that just used clapping.
> This [demonstrates] was considered a soprano clap,
> clapping two fingers together. Then we had alto clapping
> which was this [demonstrates] and bass clapping which
> was this [demonstrates]. All of us were clapping at
> different levels and the music we made was quite
> wonderful. So you can make lots and lots of different
> sounds. Other things that you can change are the louds
> and softs of sound. Constant louds can be boring, so you
> might want to vary your sound. What else can you vary?
> Speed? Yes.

> (2 November, p. 378)

Next, Johanna organized four groups of students. She began with the idea of choosing the groups herself, but after a brief discussion followed the students' request that they be allowed to choose their own groups. As the students made little circles of stools in the four corners of the room, Johanna went from group to group giving them each a single word to be represented in sound. After a few minutes, she walked around the room again and gave groups a choice of several simple instruments: a tambourine, some tapping sticks, a wind chime and so on. The groups spent about 10 minutes practising before Johanna called them back into the circle around the rug and asked which group would like to perform their sound composition first.

The first group set a jug of water on a stool on the rug, and placed a cup in it. One student held an empty test tube, another an art folio and the third student held the tambourine. Before the performance began, Johanna asked the class to close their eyes during the performance and to raise their hands when they guessed the word, rather than call out, so that they would not spoil it for other people. When Johanna signalled them to start, the group began a series of tapping, blowing, pouring and rustling sounds which told the story of the storm rising, raging and then blowing itself out. The hands shot up, and the first student Johanna asked correctly identified the sound as a storm.

The second group brought their stools into the centre of the rug. One student was holding a wind chime, another whistled, the third made some early-morning stretching sounds and the fourth made a radio alarm-clock noise. In the next two performances students represented insects and a train, the other two words Johanna had given. At the end of the performances Johanna explained that some composers had done much the same as the students had, creating sounds that told a story and suggested a musical picture. Johanna then moved across to the record-player and played a piece by Villa-Lobos called 'The Little Train of Caipira'. This is a strongly narrative piece which seems to take a train on a journey out of a station, through the countryside and brings it to rest at another station.

Johanna	What is the difference between what you guys did and Villa-Lobos did?
Michelle	It's got like elevator music in the background. It's tacky.
Johanna	So you can hear a melody in the background? That sort of tacky sound you are identifying, would 'romantic' be a good way of identifying it?
Sonya	Yeah, mushy.
Johanna	Did it start out more like yours and then change?
Christine	Yeah, it did.

45

Johanna	What they did at the beginning and what you guys did was you developed a pattern of beats. Does anyone know what that is called?
Jack	Yeah, rhythm.
Johanna	Who said that? Excellent, rhythm. When you started – what was your rhythm, remind me – that was a rhythm which made us feel the rhythm of the train. You put, as he did, several instruments in. You had your drum, your rhythm, and you had a little bit of melody over the top. [*Johanna sings the melody line of the train whistle the students had used.*] Yours came over the top like his.

(2 November, pp. 380–1)

Next, Johanna played Rimsky-Korsakov's familiar 'Flight of the Bumblebee'. After a few seconds Johanna turned down the volume temporarily, long enough for several students to call out the name of the piece. Johanna then went on to play two pieces from Grieg's *Peer Gynt*, 'Morning' and the storm sequence from 'In the Hall of the Mountain King'. Then, with only a few minutes to go Johanna made her two final teaching points, tempo and dynamics:

Johanna	The beginning, middle and end. What happens?
Michael	It starts off soft, then goes up higher like this.
Johanna	It gets higher in pitch or higher in sound level, volume?
Michael	Volume.
Johanna	Does anybody know the musical word for that?
Jacquie	Dynamic. The tension builds up while we are

waiting for the storm to break and then it
breaks and then it slows down.

Johanna   So they change both the dynamics, which is the
loudness, and they also change the speed. What
do they call the speed?

Sonya   Tempo.

Johanna   So they change the tempo of the piece. It starts
very slowly and then when it gets wild the
tempo gets fast. So they have varied that
too.

(2 November, p. 381)

With her teaching points made and the time expired, Johanna
asked the class to put their stools back under the table, to return
their musical instruments to the place they had found them,
and to move off to the morning meeting. She stood, as usual,
at the door checking the condition of the room as each student
left.

As Johanna and I walked from the art room to the morning
meeting, Johanna said, 'What are we going to do with Group 3?' The
class size and general unruliness of the group in the past few days
made repeating the success of the Group 2 lesson seem unlikely. At
break, as we sat at the staffroom table, a student came in to find out
what Johanna was teaching next period. Karen, the student, is a very
skilled musician and was often excused from attending Johanna's
rather elementary guitar lessons. Had it been guitar, her suggestion
was that she work by herself in the hall. Johanna explained that it was
music appreciation, but it occurred to me that if Karen spent some
time with the scheduled computer group it would reduce our Group
3 class size by two or three. I suggested that Karen probably knew
what Johanna was planning to teach, but Johanna was not so sure.
Whether the issue for Johanna was specific (the content of the lesson)
or general (attendance at classes), her response was to give Karen
a quick oral test on the content of the lesson. 'What is tempo?'
she asked, and 'What do we mean by *dynamics* in music?' Satisfied with Karen's responses, Johanna gave her permission to miss
the class. Karen's switch to computing, combined with a parent-led

47

knitting group which we had forgotten about, reduced the class size to under 20.

Group 3 threw themselves into the task with passion, and produced several excellent sound compositions. The noise they made while preparing their presentations, however, was absolutely dreadful. As I said to Johanna during the lesson, 'This is the sort of noise that makes me nervous when I walk down a school hallway. I always wonder what furniture is being broken inside the classroom.' It reminded me very powerfully of a drama lesson I had once taught, a lesson which was interrupted when my class noticed the principal's accusing face pressed up against the window.

Johanna followed the same lesson outline with this class as she had previously, making the same teaching points. With this class, however, the activity had the effect of doubling (quadrupling!) the already high energy level. Towards the end of the lesson, Johanna made a series of management moves designed to keep the lid on: she announced that the class was wasting time and gave a 30-second lunchtime penalty; she warned Guy and Martin that they would be excluded from the lesson next time she spoke to them; and she quietly asked Lawrence to wait outside in the hall. The only difference in the lesson plan was that towards the very end Johanna asked the whole class to lie on the floor, close their eyes, and picture the scene or story suggested by the loud and dramatic piece of music she played to them. Then she asked people to describe the scene to the class. Everyone was keen to describe what they had imagined and waited reasonably patiently while other people told their stories. Despite the madness of moments of the lesson, it worked out well. As we left the room Johanna turned to me and said: 'Phew, that was a stroke of genius, having them lie down on the floor!'

* * *

When Peter asked, 'Do we get to make animal noises too?' he was acting on the assumption that Johanna would teach the same lesson to all of her classes. Johanna did in fact teach the same lesson content using the same activities. In both cases she sat students on the floor around the rug, dropped the coins in demonstration, talked about the music which could be made with hand claps, organized students into groups for sound compositions, linked their performances with the music, and discussed the tempo and dynamics of each piece. As she had predicted before the lesson, however, the lesson was more difficult to manage with the Grade 8 class. They were more easily excited by the activities and harder to settle down for the discussion phase of the lesson, and this led Johanna to speak firmly to several students and to make one significant running change, asking students to lie quietly on the floor and then describe the scene suggested by the music she played them.

Prior to the lesson, Johanna had been aware that the lesson might be more difficult but gave no thought to changing its structure. It was, after all, an elaborate, exciting and well-practised lesson honed over the years to its present form. She was reluctant to take the easy way out and solve the problem by reducing the class size. Only after she was convinced that Karen had already mastered the material did she allow her to miss the lesson, and the further reduction due to the knitting group was out of Johanna's control. So, the difficulties that she could imagine ahead of her were solved by a combination of factors: an accidental reduction of class size, some stern words and a clear punishment at the crucial moment, and a creative, spontaneous change in the lesson plan.

LEARNING FROM EXPERIENCE

For Johanna, students' social and emotional growth is a major goal of schooling. She has several standard practices which she uses to promote this growth. One is to conduct class meetings, which may be used to solve problems the class shares,[2] or to help students learn from their experiences, as she does in 'Camping', below. Secondly, she has conferences with individuals and small groups of students, such as those in 'Conferences' (pp. 56–63). Sometimes conferences are formal and private meetings, such as the meeting with four girls who had been skipping school, and other times she catches students for brief, informal problem-solving sessions. Other less formal meetings may concern routines for recording homework due, interactions with other students, or – as is the case in the example described on pp. 60–2 – a discussion about whether a student should be allowed to discontinue instrumental music instruction. In both of these conferences, and in the class discussion in 'Camping', Johanna works hard to help students see the consequences of their actions.

Camping

This class meeting (3 October) introduced a writing assignment intended to help students in Group 2 make sense of what they learned from a school camping trip. It began with the practical details of self-sufficiency in the bush and led, unpredictably, to a discussion of the consequences of sex-role stereotyping. Johanna began, as she often does, by saying something about herself and asking a personal question of the whole class:

> I don't know about you guys but I found that the pattern
> of my sleeping in the field was that I would go to sleep
> really soundly at whatever time it was and then I would
> wake up at 3 o'clock in the morning and be wide awake.
> Did anybody else wake up in the night?

(2 October, p. 225)

This question drew a series of comments: one person managed to sleepwalk into another tent, and several girls revealed that some people had come into their tent as they were sleeping and were watching them sleep. The class was bursting to tell stories about the camp, and just as the floodgates were opening Johanna was interrupted by a student from another class who wanted to know if Johanna had any items for the morning's meeting. She mentioned several items and returned to the discussion:

> OK, the reason that I brought up this thing about
> sleeping at night was that the last night I started
> thinking about what students were actually learning
> and what I was learning by being at the camp, and the
> ways we could use it in school. I started going through
> the kinds of things I learned by doing it. I have often
> gone camping before and I have often been in the
> situation where it would have been really convenient
> for me to do the cooking, but I was scared to death

of the Coleman Stove. So, I always waited for
someone else to light it. I hated it, I was scared
to death of it, I thought it was going to blow up.
So, this was the first time that I actually had to
do it myself. It was such a feeling of independence
that I got from knowing that I could go out and start
the thing.

What I want us to do as a group here is to get with a
partner and talk about the things that you actually
learned, around ten things that you learned. It can be
things you learned about other people, things you learned
about yourself, things you learned about nature. Maybe
you really liked oatmeal! Things you learned about
your ability to survive in circumstances that are
less than pleasant. So, can you do that for me
right now.

(3 October, pp. 225–6)

Johanna helped the class to find partners, and they settled
quickly to making their lists of things they learned. As they began,
Johanna moved around the room from group to group. When she
stopped at the group I was listening to, she sat down on a stool
and asked them what they learned. The brief discussion went like
this:

Jack   Next time I should bring a sleeping bag.

Johanna   Did you learn something about the kinds of
            students you like to go camping with and the
            kinds of students that are rotten to go camping
            with?

Patrick   I learned two things.

Johanna   Good, I thought you might have learned
            something.

Satisfied that this group had now started on the right track, she
moved on to the next group. The two boys she had spoken to
continued:

Jack	I can't remember what she said, I wasn't listening. What did you learn?
Patrick	Why?
Jack	I learned never to eat with the person who cooks.
Patrick	Shall I write that down?

These boys never quite managed to rise beyond this level of minimal compliance with the task. As I listened to them, it seemed as if they found the question either foolish or embarrassing, or both. In the other groups, there seemed to be much more animation. After struggling on for a few minutes, one of the boys I had been listening to asked Johanna whether it was all right to write 'Never ask Robert to cook.' Her response was to ask what it was about Robert that made them say that.

| Jack | He cooked spaghetti and two seconds later it froze. |

Confused over the meaning of this comment, Johanna read over their shoulders:

Johanna	'Never eat with the person who cooks?' So the person who cooks the dinner shouldn't get to sit down with you? I don't understand.
Jack	OK, it's like, 'Like it . . . or die.' Never eat what the person cooks.
Johanna	Oh, so, 'Never trust another kid to cook for you?'
Jack	Right, because you never know what they are going to cook.

(3 October, pp. 226–7)

After drawing these two lads out, Johanna prepared to move off. She looked across to me and said: 'There are interesting levels of learning about this!' Plainly, the other groups she had listened to as she moved around the class were making more of the task. Next, she asked the class to finish because she was going to ask them all to share their results. The stools were pulled into the circle, and Johanna arranged several students into different places with the comment: 'When we talk together it's important that everybody can see every other face.'

When the class was arranged to her satisfaction, she asked people to tell one of the things they learned.

Jack	I learned never to eat what another person cooks.
Patrick	Never ask Robert to cook.
Holly	I learned that late nights mean awful mornings.
Natalie	It's hard to get a Coleman Stove started.

All of these comments were met with an affirming nod or a soft 'OK'. A series of other comments about hunger, cold and not being properly prepared were made. When one student, Lauren, said: 'I learned how much Mark can eat', Johanna broadened the issue to the functioning of this particular food group more generally:

Johanna	Yes, Mark's food group has some talking they have to do about what happened.
Alana	He would eat everything. We made a salad and he ate everything.
Johanna	Would it surprise you to know that his description of the camp is totally different? He sees you as not willing to do anything. Would that surprise you?
Michelle	No, not really because he told us that we didn't appreciate him. He cooked stuff the way he liked it. We had cream of chicken but he didn't put water in it. He said he liked it without water, but Paula said 'I do want water', so Paula had to go over to the tap and have her soup cold.
Johanna	So, it was really hard for you to rise above Mark?

> *Cathie*   He didn't do anything in his food group, but he
> washed our dishes, helped us to clean up, he
> was perfectly willing to clean for our group [the
> leading social group in the school].
>
> (3 October, p. 228)

Johanna returned to the business of each student in the
circle offering something they had learned until the issue of
sexism at the camp was raised. Several girls were full of praise
for one boy who had refused to join in sexist jokes about cook-
ing and cleaning which were popular with some of the boys in their
group:

> *Frances*   I learned that Raoul is quiet at school and
> stays with the guys, but when we got there he
> was really sweet and he did a lot of stuff. It
> was surprising that he wasn't one of the guys
> who was saying 'Make me breakfast, woman.'
> He just came in and said 'How many French
> toasts do you want?'
>
> *Amy*   The other guys were being really sexist to us,
> but he would help us cook and he would
> clean . . .
>
> *Frances*   And he would help us cook.
>
> *Johanna*   Oh! There's a bit of learning for you,
> guys!
>
> *Jacquie*   'A woman's place is in the kitchen' is what
> Mark was saying. But he couldn't get the pump
> out of the stove and I showed him how to get it
> out.
>
> *Johanna*   So those are two stereotypes, the woman's place
> is in the kitchen and the man is the one who
> can do the mechanical stuff. He should be able
> to figure out stuff like how the pump works.
> But those two stereotypes broke down because
> obviously men are just as capable and are very

appreciated when they do stuff like that, and a woman can deal with the mechanical stuff.

(3 October, p. 229)

Satisfied with this telling point, Johanna moved on to explain the homework assignment: writing one paragraph about an incident from each day of the camp. In order to help them, she read aloud a story about a camping expedition, a book which was presented in the form of a school notebook with journal entries. As she read aloud, she stopped at various points to ask questions intended to help students see how they could write their own stories (a problem to which I shall return in Chapter 3).

* * *

Johanna was very pleased with this lesson. It had been intended as part of a series of writing lessons related to the camping trip, which she hoped would lead to the production of an illustrated book. The particular purpose of the introductory lesson was to help students become aware that the camp may have been about more than having fun, so that when she asked them to write about the camp they would say more than just what happened each day. She began, as she often does, with a class discussion introduced by a description of what the experience was like for her. Then, she gave the pairs of students some time to think about what they had learned and make a list before she asked them to talk to the whole class. For some students this was very helpful, because they had time to rehearse some serious thoughts about the success of their food group. For others, who had more difficulty seeing beyond the practical details, Johanna had time to help them work through a more serious issue before she asked them to talk to the whole class. When she did ask people to say what they had learned, she was thus able to go round the class and ask everyone to contribute one of the things they had learned without intimidating the less articulate students who might otherwise sit silent through a class discussion. Soon enough, she struck several serious issues including the apparently selfish and unreasonable behaviour of one student and non-sexist behaviour of another.

The formula for success here seemed to include sitting the students in an intimate circle which excluded no one, allowing students to talk to a friend about the issue before they were asked to risk making a public statement, and making no public judgements about the quality of students' contributions. It is not that Johanna was equally impressed by Jack and Frances, but that she recognized that each of them needed help to bring their thoughts and feelings to the surface and to express them in public. Jack is an immature lad who would normally lack the confidence to talk in public about a relatively revealing personal issue; Frances is a very mature and confident girl who leads the high-status peer group in the school, always has something to say and in this case brought up an important and sensitive issue for the whole class to discuss.

Beside this impressive achievement, the interesting end to the original lesson – reading aloud from an attractive illustrated book of camping stories – seemed almost an anticlimax. A few days later, when Johanna was telling me that the teachers had been under some administrative pressure about their allocation of minutes per week to various subjects, she said that she found it hard to explain to outsiders that in lessons such as this she achieved all sorts of legitimate objectives while she was busy teaching music, art or writing:

> You can't tell them that my affirmative action for the
> year was done on the camping trip, or that we were doing
> women's studies while we were doing writing.

(5 October, p. 259)

Conferences

Some of Johanna's work on students' personal growth was part of the school's deliberate programme for the year, such as the class meeting which helped students to become more conscious of what they learned from the camping trip. At other times students' deviance from teachers' expectations leads to private conferences such as the following, which was called when it was discovered that four girls had missed an afternoon of school. They had travelled into the centre of the city and spent the afternoon in a shopping mall. Johanna handled this by meeting the girls behind closed doors during lunch time (18 October). She began by reminding them that they had not slipped through the school's afternoon attendance routine, and went on to describe what it had been like for her when she realized that they were absent.

> The rule is we have to contact your parents as soon
> as we know you are not here. That's our responsibility.
> And I said to myself, 'My God, what is Elise's dad
> going to say, what is Julia's mum going to say,
> what's Holly's mum going to say when I phone up
> and say your daughter is missing?' If it were my
> daughter, I would panic, especially if I thought
> my daughter wasn't going to do that kind of
> thing. I'd think something really serious had
> happened. So, you get scared, all of the adrenalin
> starts to flow. I thought, 'Can I call these
> parents?'

(18 October, p. 308)

Johanna explained she had checked all of the places they might have been in the building and had then asked whether any students knew where the girls had gone. Despite the usual reluctance to inform on fellow students, Johanna said, another student eventually told her what had happened. Once she knew that the girls had made a plan to go to the mall, she stopped worrying about their physical safety and knew that she would not have to involve the police. She still had to call their parents, however. Johanna then summarized her feelings about the incident and explained that trust was important to the way the school functioned:

> This school is based on trust, much more than other
> schools because we give you permission to be places other
> than here . . . I have to trust that you are going to go
> where you said you were going to go and be where you
> said you were going to be. Now, because we have such a
> firm emphasis on trust, my thought is that students that

57

we can't trust shouldn't be here. How do you feel about
that?

(18 October, p. 308)

Holly's reaction was that Johanna ought to continue to trust her
because this event was an aberration. She had been told by older
students that people were never caught for skipping school the last
year, and she thought that hanging out at the mall on a school day
would be fun. For Elise, the idea had also sounded like fun but she
had been overtaken by guilt.

Elise
It wasn't very fun because every time someone
looked at me I thought that they knew we were
skipping school. This one woman looked at us
and we said, 'Oh my God she's going to go to
our school and tell our teachers.' This morning
my Dad said, 'Elise, you are going to get into a
lot of trouble, so you have to face the facts and
be honest.' Every time someone on the streetcar
looked at me I thought they were going to start
screaming at me because I didn't go to school
yesterday.

Johanna
So you really felt that it wasn't worth it?

Elise
It wasn't worth it at all. I was nervous all
the time. Even if you have a good time
it's not worth it because you are so
nervous.

Johanna
So it ended up that you got your own
punishment?

Elise
And I got grounded for a week.

(18 October, p. 309)

Elise and Holly, the two Grade 7 students in the group, seemed
to have learned something from the experience. Whether it was fun
or not, it had turned out not to be worth the guilt and embarrassment
of being caught. The two Grade 8 girls involved were much less

forthcoming, so Johanna summarized what she had heard Elise say and asked whether that was the feeling more generally:

> My feeling about trying something like this is that everybody has to try stuff in order to learn. It sounds to me from what I just heard Elise say that she learned something about herself. She can't do something that she thinks is wrong and enjoy it, because the guilt is there while she is doing it. To me that's the best learning here. I feel that's what she needed to learn. I assume that having learned that, I am going to be able to trust her. I don't know whether the same goes for the three of you.
>
> (18 October, p. 309)

Julia, the more worldly of the two Grade 8 students, was not as discomforted by the breach of trust involved or the embarrassment of being caught.

> *Johanna* Do you also agree with what Elise said or do you have different feelings about it?
>
> *Julia* Partially.
>
> *Johanna* You didn't feel so much guilt? You were easier while you were out yesterday afternoon?
>
> *Julia* Yes.
>
> *Johanna* Do you understand my concern, Julia, about students who are here needing to be students I can trust? Do you understand that as a teacher, if I give you permission to go somewhere and I think that there is a possibility that you are going somewhere else, that I am morally responsible for your safety? How are you going to show me that I can trust you?
>
> *Julia* I don't know what you want me to say. For me, trust comes with time.
>
> (18 October, pp. 309-10)

Although all four girls looked quite shaken by this interview, Julia was not willing to make the sort of public disavowal of her actions that Elise had. She did not contest the fairness of the punishment – that the time missed would have to be made up – but nor did she take the easy way out and offer an insincere apology. Johanna decided to let Julia's reaction pass and excused the tearful and shamefaced group from the meeting. For some of the other girls, the meeting had struck a more responsive chord, as the note we later found on the staffroom table indicated:

Dear Johanna, Miles and Freida:

We don't expect this letter to make up for what we did, but we just wanted to say that we learned our lesson. After our meeting we agreed that we were sorry and it wasn't worth it. We spent the whole time worrying about getting into trouble instead of how wrong it was. We didn't even consider that you might be worried. We hope that you will trust us again, because we know you can.

Yours truly,

Alana and Holly.

The next day (19 October) Johanna and I were sitting in the open area trying to work out what to do about the science programme, when a disagreement between a student and an itinerant music teacher led to another problem-solving conference. The music teacher stormed into the room and announced that, 'According to Geoffrey, he has now quit strings.' What was Johanna going to do about it? Johanna told the music teacher that she would handle it, and asked him to send Geoffrey in to see her. When Geoffrey arrived, she asked him to sit beside her and explain what had happened.

Johanna   Geoffrey, my love, tell me the news. You sound a bit discouraged.

Geoffrey   Yeah, I am discouraged, I don't like being in strings. Last year I liked it, this year I don't.

Johanna	Does it have to do with the violin?
Geoffrey	No, I still like the violin, but I don't feel like playing it here.
Johanna	Something about this group?
Geoffrey	Kind of, but I just don't really want to play.
Johanna	Sonya is the first violin, I guess. Is Dale as good as Sonya? Are they as good as Ben and Dean last year? Is it because the group isn't as good as last year?
Geoffrey	No, but I just don't like the way it turned about this year.

(19 October, pp. 325-6)

Having checked the possibility that Geoffrey was discouraged by the standard of other players, Johanna moved on to discuss the consequences of deciding to withdraw from strings. In particular, she knew that the decision might lead to problems for him at home. His parents had bought him an expensive violin which they said they would return to the store if he did not practise consistently.

Johanna	Do you understand what the consequence of that decision is going to be in terms of the violin your parents bought?
Geoffrey	Yes.
Johanna	So, you have decided you don't ever want to have a good violin, or what do you think?
Geoffrey	If I take it up again it will be at high school.
Johanna	Will they supply you with a violin?
Geoffrey	Yes.
Johanna	So you are just basically taking a break for this year, and that is going to sit OK with your parents?

> *Geoffrey*   I don't know what they are going to do,
> but I don't really care because it is up
> to me.
>
> *Johanna*   So this is a decision you can make, and you feel
> that they are not going to put pressure on you.
> OK, well you sort it out, it sounds OK
> to me.
>
> (19 October, p. 326)

* * *

Both of these discussions began as disciplinary issues, and in both cases Johanna's response was to put aside the issue of rules and to focus instead on two other aspects: feelings and consequences. In Geoffrey's case, the music teacher had been enraged by what he saw as insolence and wilfulness: what right did a 13-year-old have to tell him that he wanted no further part in his class? Instead of responding to this issue, Johanna asked Geoffrey to talk about his feelings about continuing in strings and the consequences for him of leaving. When she had checked that the issue was not something she could help him with – discouragement about the standard of playing in the group – she moved on to explore the consequences for Geoffrey of leaving the group. She knew that there was some family history behind the decision, and once she knew that Geoffrey had thought about the serious family consequences of his withdrawal from strings she let his decision stand. The initial issue of discipline, the supposed insult to the music teacher, was the least of Johanna's or Geoffrey's problems in this discussion and was allowed to pass without further comment.

In the conference with the girls who had preferred the shopping mall to school, Johanna also began by moving away from the disciplinary issue to consider the feelings involved and the consequences of their actions. Had it occurred to them that people might have been worried about their safety? Had they thought of the breaches of trust involved? Was it worth it, after all? Although this conversation was conducted in the personal problem-solving format Johanna used with Mark and Geoffrey, the tone of the conversation was much more tense. Students might, for example, have heard only the implied threat in what she was saying (' . . . students who are here [need] to be students I can trust'). Although Elise, Holly and Alana seemed to be genuinely remorseful, Julia was unwilling to make a public apology. Her refusal to respond to Johanna's request that she show her that she was worthy of trust challenged Johanna's construction of the issue. She had skipped school, enjoyed it and been caught, and was now going to be punished. Trust was another matter, something that could be won – or lost – over time, and not something that could be guaranteed by a formula apology. Johanna chose to let the challenge pass, rather than contest the issue and turn the meeting into a test of strength.

The external problem-solving form of this discussion masks a teacher–student disciplinary confrontation. Johanna did not explicitly threaten students or raise her voice, and she did help some of the students to understand more about the consequences of their actions. Nevertheless, the meeting was founded on the conventional asymmetry of power between students and teachers. Johanna was legally responsible for their safety and she wanted these and other students to know that they could not slip through the cracks of the school's attendance system. She had been genuinely concerned about their safety, and she recognized that 'people have to try stuff out to learn', but she had also been pleased to have caught some students so early in the year. Like anyone charged with maintaining the boundaries of behaviour of a group, Johanna was pleased that some reasonably impressionable and influential people had been caught breaking the rules so early in the year. As she said to Miles in the staffroom a few minutes later, 'It was perfect, we got the right kids to do it.'

SUMMARY AND CONCLUSIONS

In these lessons, the temporal quality of understanding teaching is clear. Johanna's past, present and the future run together. In order for us to understand the present of these stories fully it is necessary to look both behind and beyond the surface patterns: look behind the stories for the history which shaped them, and beyond the stories to the predispositions to future action they represent. Describing the present alone is insufficient. As Gadamer (1975, p. 321) puts it:

> 'To recognize what is' does not mean recognizing what is
> just at this moment there, but to have insight into the
> limitations within which the future is open to expectation
> and planning. . . . Thus true experience is that of one's
> own historicality.

What is 'just at this moment there' in the present of these stories is
a series of patterns of teaching and some particular pieces of educational content. One way of understanding these familiar patterns
would be to separate out and name a series of categories or domains
of knowledge.[3] The difficulty with such an analysis is its distance
from Johanna's own understanding of her teaching. For her, teaching
does not exist as routines and rhythms, or rules of practice and practical principles. Her knowledge is more like a cornucopia, a mixture
of tricks, stock phrases, places to draw the line, concepts, and ways
of speaking to people which spill out in a different assortment in each
lesson. For this reason, I have preferred to use the catch-all term
'patterns' in describing the mixture of recurring events in her
lessons.

Some of Johanna's patterns of teaching are fixed and present on almost every occasion she teaches. She usually stands
at the door at the end of a lesson and asks people whether their
table captain has dismissed them, and she usually begins class
discussions by relating some personal experience of her own. Other
patterns have been developed to match the needs of particular
subjects; her system of allocating guitars and of singing along
as students play the chords, for example. Still other patterns concern her use of the blue oriental rug in the centre of the art room as
the physical focus of activities: a place to display coloured fishes;
to perform pictures with music; or to gather around for a class
meeting.

Her patterns of teaching allow Johanna to resolve familiar
classroom problems in ways that are comfortable for her. Johanna's
pattern of gathering people in a circle around the rug for class discussions, for example, was used in 'Fishes', 'Fastwurms' and 'Camping'.
Johanna involves everyone in class discussions by asking people to
gather in closely together, by ensuring that no one sits outside the circle and by insisting that she be able to see every face. She helps people
to make contributions to the discussion by using small groups to

ensure that people are not too intimidated to speak in the large
group, by working her way round the circle when she is sure
that everyone will have something to contribute, and by acknowledging but not judging the comments students make. These patterns in her class discussions allow her to teach in a warm
and friendly environment and they help students explore the
issues which press in on them in adolescence. More than this,
her clear expectations of appropriate behaviour in class discussions limit the possibility that Johanna will have to deal
with the 'craziness' of some of the lessons in the school's open
area.

This class discussion pattern, and other patterns she uses,
provides Johanna with ways of organizing the class which may
be matched to a variety of content. In 'Fishes', Johanna used
a class discussion format to explain the concept of 'value' in
graphics. In 'Fastwurms' she used the class discussion to help
people understand a challenging visit to an art gallery. In 'Camping',
the content of the lesson came from Johanna's attempt to help
students learn from the experience of camping out, being away
from home, and having to organize and prepare food together in
groups.

The sources of the content Johanna uses are various. Some of it,
the concepts in art theory and music appreciation she teaches, for
example, come from the parent academic disciplines. In 'Fishes', the
art theory is chosen in the hope that it will help students make more
of a current school activity, the displays following the visit to
the farmers' market. The discussion following the gallery visit in
'Fastwurms', on the other hand, came from Johanna's current personal interests and her belief that it is important that people
learn to appreciate the beauty around them. In 'Camping' and
'Conferences', Johanna was pursuing learning goals which are central to her hopes and dreams for education, helping students
to understand who they are and how they may grow to become
independent and responsible adults. Her judgements about what
is relevant and useful to teach, then, are neither shaped nor constrained by school board guidelines in the subjects she teaches.
Instead she matches the needs and interests she sees around her
with content and patterns of teaching she carries forward from year
to year.

Behind these patterns and their educational content stand Johanna's biography and experience. The patterns are not arbitrary: they represent Johanna's best solutions to the practical problems she faces in the classroom. To take the example of her guitar teaching, represented here by 'Fingers Like Hammers', the patterns she uses solve an elaborate set of practical problems in a way which is consistent with her sense of herself as a teacher in general and a music teacher in particular. Johanna once told me that giving a full class of students a guitar each is a bit like giving them each a machine gun. It is inevitable that they are going to wave them about, play with them, pretend to know how to use them, and see what sort of noises they can make. The trick for Johanna has been to find a way of them all having a guitar without anyone getting shot. She does not want to have to be authoritarian about the need to be silent when she is giving an explanation, nor does she want to have to badger and remind them, but she must have complete silence while she is tuning, demonstrating or making a point. The way in which she does this was learned in the years she taught music full time, repeating each lesson as many as seven or eight times a week. After years of practice, Johanna has now refined the whole-class guitar lesson to the point where she is confident that she can handle any of the problems that are likely to emerge:

> I have learned how to do a guitar lesson that works. All
> the possible behaviors that kids can throw at me around
> guitar have happened, I have dealt with them, and now it
> happens successfully. . . . Almost always, because there's
> always one kid who will surprise you. Almost always I
> can account for what is going to happen. That's where
> the experience counts. I'm comfortable and I do a good
> job.
>
> (8 November, p. 416)

Her patterns of teaching have reduced the number of problems she has to deal with, and they do so in a way that is consistent with her sense of herself as a teacher. Her limited formal training in music, which reduces the possibility that she could have become what she calls a 'minor scales' music teacher, combined with her belief that her task is to introduce all students to the pleasure of music-making, means that she values the confidence and participation of the many more than the excellence of the few. She knows, from her own experience as an adult learner, how easily beginning musicians may be discouraged from participation and she is dedicated above all else to ensuring that no one becomes discouraged from making music by her guitar lessons.

The final point to be made here is that when Johanna is working deftly on lessons in her repertoire she solves the practical problems of teaching so well that they become almost invisible. In most of the stories in this chapter there is no sense that the forces of entropy are going to drag the lesson down into chaos, or that she has had to work hard to motivate, control or discipline students. She recognizes that the Grade 8 class is harder than the Grade 7 classes to teach, but she doesn't plan to behave any differently as a result. Preferring to teach what she believes is right, she trusts that she will spontaneously solve whatever problems emerge. In 'Pictures With Music', for example, she used a few stern words at the beginning of the lesson and just when the lesson threatened to spin out of control asked students to lie quietly on the floor and listen to the music. In 'Fishes', when her classroom jokes threatened the equilibrium she had established, she quickly reasserted her control.

Although Johanna does not see herself as part of the mainstream of teaching, she sees some differences between herself and other teachers in alternative schools. Her classroom control is mostly invisible, submerged in the patterns of teaching she has developed, but Johanna gently maintains firm control over her students. She tells students where to sit for particular lessons, insists on absolute attention during guitar lessons, carefully marshals who shall speak next in her class discussions, but rarely has any cause to show irritation or to raise her voice. In the most delicate of her interactions with students, in meetings such as those described in 'Conferences', her control is even more muted. She is subtle and delicate in her use of authority. Her actions are guided by the belief that learning is more likely within a safe and controlled environment:

> *Johanna*   Part of [my] understanding of learning is that it can only happen in a situation where there is agreement to participate in it. In a situation where there is no control, where the students are not exhibiting any self-control, there's no agreement to go ahead with learning. . . .
>
> *Bill*   That might not be universally shared by teachers in alternative schools.
>
> *Johanna*   Yes there are some who prefer to allow kids to experience the depth of despair . . .
>
> (8 November, p. 419)

Johanna's repertoire, that stock of refined and practised lessons which form the experiential basis for the new lessons she invents each day, has been represented by six stories in this chapter. These lessons from her repertoire are little jewels, formed under the weight of years of experience, cut and sharpened to a perfect shape over the years, and polished freshly each time they are taught. Considered together, these stories provide a sense of the kinds of pattern of teaching Johanna has practised, the sources of the content she usually draws from, and the particular kind of invisible control she strives for in her lessons. These qualities, I have argued, are not just a pattern in the ethnographic present but are a historically shaped predisposition to act in the future. Teaching is an uncertain activity: the relationships between teachers and students change, forces outside the classroom propel teachers in new directions, and teachers are thrown into unfamiliar subject areas. The next two chapters, 'Writing' and 'Science' will explore what happens to Johanna's repertoire when she is confronted with the task of teaching two unfamiliar subjects.

NOTES

1. Quotations such as these, transcribed from my audio-tapes into daily field notes, are identified by the date and page number of the original field records.

2. See the example described in 'This Is Rubbish', Chapter 3, pp. 89–100.
3. Such categories might include: routines (Yinger, 1979 and Leinhardt *et al.* 1987); rules of practice and practical principles (Elbaz, 1983); rhythms (Clandinin and Connelly, 1986); principles, maxims and norms (Shulman, 1986).

Chapter 3

Writing

This chapter describes the extension of Johanna's repertoire to include new patterns of teaching in the subject of writing. Whereas in the lessons described in Chapter 2 Johanna was teaching from a polished and practised set of patterns and content which resolved the most familiar problems she faced, this chapter shows how the new demands of teaching writing exposed unfamiliar practical problems which pressed for resolution and which required her to master new content knowledge. The major argument to be made here is that Johanna's repertoire is constantly in the process of formation. Confronted by new problems, she adds new content and patterns of teaching which reflect the biography and experience she brings to those problems. In this series of writing lessons she adds new patterns and content with relative ease because they were consistent with the biographical imperatives she brought to teaching and with the repertoire she already had.

During the lessons described in this chapter Johanna's students wrote, designed and bound their own illustrated books. I had expected to continue in these lessons as I had before, watching and helping while Johanna taught art. My interest in the teaching of writing, however, led to an unexpected expansion in the first phase of the illustrated book project, writing the text for each book, and my role changed from a peripheral participant-observer to an equal collaborator in teaching all three of Johanna's classes. The change in my role was an important development in the study. Once I began teaching I realized that I was gaining access to a new kind of information about the problem of understanding teaching. In addition to attempting to reconstruct Johanna's understanding and reflection, I was now able to describe my own understanding of teaching and some of the changes in this understanding over time. I began to rediscover my own repertoire as a teacher, a repertoire which I thought I might have lost in five years' absence from teaching, and I realized that it was changing under Johanna's influence. The risk I took in teaching Johanna's classes provided a powerful force for symmetry in our partnership. Johanna had earlier been concerned that I would sit in judgement on her mistakes, and so it seemed much fairer that she should have opportunities to see the imperfections in my own teaching practice.

From a sequence of more than thirty writing lessons with each of these classes, I have chosen to tell four stories: how the lesson sequence began with Johanna's uncertainty about how best to help students to write grammatically correct texts, 'Do You Think They Learned Anything?'; a pair of writing conferences with students, 'Talking about Writing'; a crisis in which we confronted our lack of success with Group 3, 'This Is Rubbish'; and the final phase of the book project, when we had achieved an apparently effortless, productive atmosphere which satisfied both of us, 'Finishing Up'. In the final section, 'Summary and Conclusions', I will return to a description of the changes in Johanna's practice during these lessons, a process of change which I will characterize as 'fusion of horizons'.

DO YOU THINK THEY LEARNED ANYTHING?

Following the school's annual four-day camping trip, Johanna had asked all three of her classes to write a paragraph about each day. After collecting and reading these pieces of writing, she decided that it would be helpful to work with the students on punctuation and sentence construction. Her lesson plan (11 October) involved correcting a piece she had borrowed from a student's camping-trip notes and modified for her own purposes. She had the piece typed with some 18 intentional punctuation errors and asked students in all three classes to make the corrections. The two Grade 7 lessons were fluid, lively and well received by the students, but Johanna encountered some resistance from the Grade 8 class. This was not surprising, as she had been struggling with this group. Although they completed the task as they had been asked to, and seemed to enjoy doing so, Johanna had to stop the lesson several times to ensure that they were all on task. She seemed to be working quite hard and getting much less than her usual pleasure from teaching.

Later in the day we were talking about how different our perceptions of the Grade 8 classes have been. For example, I had been very satisfied with an extremely carefully planned science class I taught to the Grade 8s the previous week, although I knew that students' lack of commitment had made Johanna nervous at some points. From my own perspective, the level of disorder in the science lesson was a pale shadow of the chaos possible in a lesson involving lots of fragile glassware and messy liquids.[1] In the case of this punctuation lesson, I suggested to Johanna that she had been unduly concerned about the issue of control. I had been sitting on the edge of a group of relatively 'squirrelly' students, people Johanna had spoken to several times, and had noticed that they had all actually enjoyed completing the task. They had done the corrections, listened closely while Johanna called out the answers, and taken a close interest in how many of the errors they had located. Considered in terms of the students' satisfaction with completing the task, I thought that the lesson was reasonably successful.

Johanna was reluctant to agree, and shifted her concern to whether students had learned anything from the lesson:

> Do you think they learned anything from that? I
> realized at the end that for the students who do
> not know what a sentence is, telling them where the
> period goes is not going to teach them. . . . What
> am I trying to think of with these guys? I see a
> need to do sentence diagrams with these students, for
> them to take the language apart and see how it
> all fits together. Now, I happen to have done a
> lot of this as a kid and it seemed to stand me in
> good stead in that I can pull apart any sentence
> and tell you where a phrase is connected. That might
> be what they need. What do people who write
> think about that these days?

(11 October, pp. 279–80)

As a former writing teacher, I had lots of thoughts on this issue. I explained that there was some divergence of opinion but that I did not see much value in structural analysis except for the most accomplished writers. Johanna asked me what I would do instead of sentence diagrams.

Johanna	How do you help them with their writing of stories, and give them a feeling of success?
Bill	The first thing I would do would be give them quite a lot of very silent time. I wouldn't ask them to write at home.
Johanna	No?
Bill	Because it is hard for students to find half an hour at home where it is quiet. Some will, but I would make sure that they had the experience of, 'There's forty minutes of quiet time. Bill and I will be coming around to help you, but I want you to think and write but not to talk.' I would encourage them to write as much as they could, like: 'I want to see everyone write three pages.' Or something quite arbitrary and almost unattainable. So that would be the first thing I would do.
Johanna	Would you have them think about any structure for it, where their story might be going, or are you just going to have them write?
Bill	My instinct is to leave the structure until they have some text to play with. One of the biggest problems is getting started and getting enough done. Students get so critical of what they have done, they say, 'This is stupid, I can't do this.' You get a lot of that kind of resistance. I give a lot of resistance to myself when I am writing, so one way of overcoming my own resistance is never to start with the first paragraph. I think, 'What's the easiest place I can start with here?'

(11 October, pp. 281–2)

HAROLD BRIDGES LIBRARY
S. MARTIN'S COLLEGE
LANCASTER

73

What I was saying appealed to Johanna, so she asked me to say something along these lines to her classes next time we had writing. During the next two days I had no time to think about what I would do, as I was overtaken by a bureaucratic crisis which temporarily threatened the continuation of the study. The very next time I thought of what to do was when I was confronted by a Grade 7 writing class two days later. Then I taught two writing lessons, virtually identical in structure. The lesson described here was the second lesson, with the Grade 8 students in Group 3.

The lesson began, as usual, with some difficulty about lateness after the morning break. As we were eventually 10 minutes late starting, 5 minutes beyond the deadline Johanna has set, Johanna insisted that whole class make up the lost 5 minutes at lunch time. She introduced me as an 'expert writing teacher' and, despite the difficult start, I began my part of the lesson full of sweet reason. Speaking softly, I gave a 5-minute monologue on the experience of writing, before I asked students to begin their own writing:

OK. [*Very softly*] The way I want to start today is to tell
you a bit about what I do when I write. Right now, my
job is that I am a full-time writer. I come into the school
in the mornings and . . . Jenny, I am not going to raise
my voice to talk over yours, and I want you to listen to
what I have to say. [*She rolls her eyes.*] And you can roll
your eyes if you like, but I still want you to listen. What
I was saying is that I spend about half of every day
writing, so I have a good sense of what it is like to write
at the moment. I wanted to talk to you a bit about how I
do my writing, and then make a link between how I write
and some of your writing.

When I came in this morning I sat down and started
writing about what had happened to me yesterday,
when I thought that this research project was going
to be stopped. I just wrote whatever came into my mind.
So, you end up with a bit of scruffy writing like this.

(13 October, p. 293)

Then I spread some of my handwritten field notes and completed typescript out on the rug in the centre of the room where everyone could compare the disorganized first draft with the neat, thick and (superficially) impressive print-out of the completed field notes. I emphasized that I had produced hundreds of pages of similar stories about the school by beginning with 'whatever came into my mind':

> The point I want to make is that I didn't start by thinking, 'What is the most important thing that happened in the day', or 'How do I want to start this story', or 'What's the point of the story going to be'? I just started by writing down the very first thing that came into my mind. This is the way I do it: wherever there is a place to start, I start. Then, the next day or weekend I look back at the notes I have made, just scruffy notes like this and ask myself, 'What's the story that these notes are telling me?' Then, I have another complete go at writing them.
>
> Now, I want to encourage you to write like that because one of the main problems with writing, especially in school, is that people feel that what they do isn't good enough. They think it will be full of mistakes, people won't like it, that it will be 'dumb'. I want to help you to get through that stage. The way I do it is I make sure that I get a lot of silence. I get a quiet place, where there isn't a television, there isn't someone unwrapping their lunch [*a reference to someone in the class*] and I make myself sit still in that silent place until I have built up a few pages. So, that's what I am going to get you to do today.
>
> In order to help you get started on that what I am going to get you do is take out a fresh piece of paper and write whatever comes into your mind. [*Rustling of pages and whispering begins.*] Now [*raising voice*], just before you start, the way I said I was going to help you is to make sure you have room to write and you don't get interrupted. So, if you are at a table where there are too many people, that table that Lance is at might have one

too many people, make sure you have a space in front of
you and take out a piece of paper.

(13 October, pp. 293–4)

At this point there was a series of questions about what to write,
what sort of paper to use and so forth. I moved around the room checking that everyone had the materials to start and that they realized
that they had to start now. After 2 minutes, during which about
half of the students began to settle to work but there was still a
babble of background noise, I called the whole class back to attention. The reaction of the class was not instantaneous, and I stood
waiting in the middle of the room wearing my long-suffering look.
Almost immediately, Johanna chipped in.

Johanna	Taking a long time guys . . .
Bill	OK, now that everyone has a piece of paper and a pencil I am going to repeat the instruction in case you were only partly listening. When I stop, I want you just to write in silence. You will be working right through to lunch time. Johanna and I are here to help you, so if you are stuck, can't get started, put your hand up and we'll come around and help you. Just a reminder, we are thinking about a story which takes place on the camping trip but it could be about camping in general, it could be about a time when you were in a canoe and it turned over. Write as much as you can, don't censor what you are writing, just get started. If you are really stuck, just write, 'Maybe I could write this, maybe I could write that.'

(13 October, p. 295)

Immediately, six or eight hands shot up, but I did not respond
to their questions. Instead, I said that Johanna and I would come
around up the class and answer questions one by one. As I went

around the class I stopped people erasing their first attempts or throwing pieces of paper away, explaining that I found I didn't always know which were the good bits so I didn't throw my first starts away. When people could not find a place to start I suggested that they write down the questions they had. With another student, I asked if there was ever a time she had been really frightened, and suggested that she write about that. I read over their shoulders, praised students for the amount that they had written, and pointed out pieces I particularly liked. All this was done in whispers, as the class continued to work in complete silence for the remaining 40 minutes of the lesson.

As the time drew to a close I began to read the pieces. Where there was a strong line of action but no description, I suggested that students choose a moment and say what they could see and hear at that moment and what was going on inside them. When a moment was already described in some detail, I asked for some thoughts about what sort of story might surround that moment. When there was less to work with I just asked students to choose the sentence or paragraph they liked best and to say why. Once they started, the class worked without resistance, and for longer than I had known them to in the past. They seemed surprised and pleased at how much they had been able to produce, and I was able to do some useful one-to-one teaching for the first time with this group.

* * *

When Johanna asked, 'Do you think they learned anything?' she grasped one of the horns of an essential dilemma in teaching: the issue of education and social control.[2] This particular formulation of the issue, borrowed from Sharp and Green's (1975) book title, is one of the many faces it wears. In 'Johanna's Story', for example, the dilemma is formulated in terms of independence: her educational goal is to help students learn to be independent, but some of the school's *laissez-faire* practices such as 'independent time' conflict with her expectations of order and control.

My description of the sentence-structure lesson focused on control: whether the small group of students I sat with were busy. In this class, which we had not found easy to teach, I judged the lesson a success because the students knew what to do and seemed satisfied with

77

their own work. My guess was that they found the task of correcting punctuation on a handout familiar, obviously legitimate for a teacher to set, and – best of all – easy to do and get right. Johanna had to stop the lesson several times to ensure complete attention but this seemed to me to be well within the ordinary range of teachers' control of classes.

Johanna's question about what they *learned* attended to the other, educational, horn of the education–control dilemma. Unfamiliar with the problem of teaching writing, Johanna's first thought was to look back at her own schooling for models of teaching. When she had been at school, teachers had taught parsing of sentences. As she said, this seemed to have worked well for her. I, too, was taught English in this way but when she asked me 'What do people . . . think about that these days?' I looked to my experience as a teacher rather than as a student. As a teacher I had learned that only the most able language users' writing benefited from these sorts of exercise. Although completion of the exercises often gave most students a feeling of success, their subsequent written work did not seem to reflect the lessons I set out to teach. My response to Johanna, however, was not to lay out my thinking, to recount my experience, or to refer to the research I have read or polemics I have written on the subject, but to describe in practical terms what I would do instead.

Johanna's interest in my description threw me into a familiar teaching task. As a teacher, I also had to deal with the education–control dilemma. Initially supported by Johanna's authority, uninvolved in the skirmish over lateness, and introduced as an expert, I began as if my only concerns were educational. Within seconds, however, I was responding to the class as a teacher rather than a visiting speaker, demanding silence and attention and setting expectations about which kinds of question I was willing to answer and when. These teacherly responses were drawn without thinking from my distant past and seemed to lead to an appropriate resolution to the education–control dilemma in this lesson. The class did something educationally useful by my standards, and they had worked more quietly and energetically than they had in the earlier writing lesson. Like Johanna's well-polished art and music lessons, this lesson came directly from my practised repertoire.

At lunch time that day, Johanna asked me to talk about the second writing lesson. She was particularly interested in what I thought we should do next. After months of asking her to talk about her actions and intentions, I was nonplussed when I found the metaphorical boot on the other foot. It did not seem quite natural to think ahead about what I would do next. Left to my own devices I would have given it no further thought until the class was in front of me again. Asked to think about it, of course, I was able to say something about what I would do and why, so I laid out some of my thinking about teaching writing:

> The next step would be to ask them to do something with
> the piece they had written. This probably means that I
> would get them to read back over it and tick the parts
> they liked, or choose the part they were going to go on
> with. Alternatively, I might ask them to choose a person
> to read their work and give some advice on what to do
> next. For some students, only the teachers would be safe
> enough to choose for this activity. The key thing would
> be to move them on to another draft, after making a
> selection from their notes. The stage after that would be
> to get them to write more carefully, perhaps by asking
> them to write on every second line of the paper and
> using loose sheets. These could then be edited and
> proofed through several stages without the tedium of
> rewriting. Finally, they should prepare some kind of
> perfect copy for display or as the text of their picture
> books.

(13 October, pp. 298-9)

Transformed by this lesson from an observer to a teacher, I also realized that my understanding of teachers' knowledge might be further explored by interrogating my own experience of teaching at Community School. I noticed that Johanna had been trying to work out what I was doing during my lesson and had made some notes of her own on loose-leaf paper, so that night I wrote some notes about the thinking behind what I had been doing. It was no trouble to deconstruct this teaching process and explain why the decisions were taken, but as I wrote the note I was aware that I had no consciousness of the reasons informing my action at the time. For example:

- a long quiet introduction has a soothing effect on students who have come in late and noisy;
- questions represent resistance to the task and must be cut off reasonably quickly before they ruin the tone that has been set;
- instructions inevitably have to be repeated for some students, but are better repeated individually than holding the class up beyond a certain point;
- individual differences among writers mean that desk supervision is the essential teaching time – sitting at the desk and marking would be a sin;
- even the most reluctant person can write about a time they were really scared;
- and so on.

(13 October, p. 297)

This list represents some of the tacit knowledge behind my taken-for-granted actions. Now that I was teaching again, it felt as if I was doing what comes naturally. I had no conscious sense of where the lesson was going next, but no reason to be concerned. Wherever the lesson went, it would be to a place I knew and understood. As Dickens might have put it, we were now in the presence of the ghost of lessons past and the ghost of lessons yet to come.

TALKING ABOUT WRITING

In the Grade 7 classes, our joint writing lessons fell into an easy pattern. Johanna would begin the lesson by introducing the next step in the process of book production – drawing sketches, making a dummy book, choosing a medium for the illustrations, cutting correct-sized pages, and so on – and then we would both move around the room helping students with either their writing or their art. The two episodes which make up the next story show the kinds of conversation we were having as we circled around each class. In the first vignette, Johanna listened to me as I discussed a script with a student (7 November), and in the second she used her own version of the same practice (11 November).

On 7 November we had three writing lessons. During the Group 1 lesson, Johanna called me over to Natalie's table to read her story. She had been trying to help Natalie, but had encountered some resistance to making any changes. Johanna wanted me to talk to her, and to listen in case I came up with anything that would move her. In front of Natalie, she asked me to read the story and give Natalie some advice.

Johanna	When I first read Natalie's story it was lacking in a lot of adjectives.
Bill	It was flat, was it?
Johanna	Then I read the second part, which was absolutely the opposite. It was full of lovely adjectives. I said could Natalie go back and add adjectives to make it read more like this and then think of something that might tie the stories together. She had no idea how to do it. She hasn't been able to write something that ties it up. So I'm not sure how further to help her.
Bill	Can I have a read, Natalie?
Natalie	Be my guest. You may get stuck on the second page because it's sort of weird.
Bill	It's sort of weird? Well I've seen a few weird stories in my time so it won't shock me. [*Reads.*] Well, I can see one way of unifying it. It seems to me you've told two quite similar stories, one about the sunrise and one about the stars. One of the things I would do with a story like that is I would take those two ideas out and put them in the title, so if you call the thing something like . . . 'Sunrise and stars', for example, it organizes the reader in the beginning to look for this in the story. That's

	one step. The second step is to make more of the idea that it was very peaceful and it gave you lots of time for contemplation. Right?
Natalie	Where would I do that?
Bill	What I am going to suggest is that you write that in somewhere for the reader. That's the feeling I get reading it. For you the favourite parts were very peaceful and contemplative and enjoying nature and all that sort of stuff. That's what you are telling me, isn't it?
Natalie	Yeah.
Bill	OK, here are several suggestions. I would take out this sentence here because if you finish with this it would be an anticlimax. It tells the reader straight out what he or she is supposed to be feeling. This second last sentence is a much better place to end. Leave us with the feeling not with a summary of the feeling. Also, I would try and find some way of linking them together. You will need to go back to the beginning of the story and make it less, 'This happened and that happened and that happened' and more . . .
Natalie	Descriptive?
Bill	Well the description is very good but the point of the story is not so much that these things happened but that you want to communicate the feeling you had when these things happened.
Johanna	You might do a little stage setting.
Natalie	So take out the 4 a.m. and put 'early'.
Bill	Yes, that kind of fine detail sounds more like a scientific report but it is kind of distracting. What Johanna is suggesting is the thing I think you should think about and perhaps talk

to us about tomorrow. The advice Johanna is giving you is that you need to set the scene more, getting the reader prepared for the idea that the camping trip allowed you to have these particular lovely experiences. You have ended up here on this point, but you should prepare for it more. OK?

(7 November, pp. 402–4)

In the same class a few days later (11 November), I overheard Johanna having a similar kind of discussion with Holly. By now, everyone in Group 1 except Holly had the texts of their illustrated books completed and checked. Johanna and I had been moving around the room in our familiar rhythm, this time helping students with the layout and illustration of their books. While the other 15 students in the class were busy painting, cutting paper, making up dummy books and sketching, Johanna spent ten minutes working with Holly's typed first draft of her story. Holly is a reluctant writer who receives learning assistance. She originally needed a lot of help to get started, had some trouble with her first draft, and had missed several days of school since then. The story was a computer print-out version of the handwritten piece she had been working on for five or six lessons. Johanna began by reading the story aloud. (The text of Holly's story as Johanna read it aloud appears in italics.)

Johanna   [Reading] *I looked at the luggage that was piled up neatly against the wall and wondered if four bags were enough and with a sigh decided it was. Just then the phone rang. It was for me.*
           Perfect beginning paragraph.
           'Hello,' I said in a cheery voice. It was Sarah. She wanted to make sure everything was ready for tomorrow. It was going to be a great two days. She made sure I knew where to meet and other boring details. After I hung up I decided to make sure I had all my food. Each

83

person was in charge of bringing certain food. I got junk food.

OK. This needs work, but it is fine. Basically what is in it is fine. We are going to work on making this a little bit clearer because this is hard for me to understand. This part about 'each person was in charge', we'll work on that. You did this on computer? Is there any way you can print it out with double spacing?

Two packages of marshmallows ...

This is wonderful. It is so obviously an absolute pig-out. It's just perfect.

'But is it enough?' I thought. It would have to be.

So, the junk food, it's funny, because you have obviously got enough. Not even thirty students could eat that much junk food in two days, so you have sort of made a joke of it. It's cute.

The next day we talked all of the way to the campgrounds. Let me tell you that's not easy, to talk and ride a bike at the same time, but we managed to do it extremely well.

OK. I want another sentence in here I think. Something tells me you need a little bit more detail. When I am reading it's not clear to me whether you got driven to the campgrounds or what is happening until I get to the very end of this page and then it is too late. So I would like some more info about how you got there.

My Dad was already there and we started to pitch our tents ... Thank God my Dad agreed to bring up our luggage, gear and food.

This is a sort of strange way to do it, to have the students biking together and then meet their parents to set up the campsite. It might be an idea to put in what the plan was before you get to actually doing it. OK? So where could you put what is going on? [*Holly points out a place.*] OK, 'It was going to be a great two days.' Now, 'the other boring details' might be a good place to put that in. So give us a few boring details, like we were going to bike to a campsite, to spend two days there. Why were you going to the campsite? To get to know each other better? What were you trying to do?

Holly   To get away on our own for the weekend and have a good time.

Johanna   So, put in that kind of stuff up to 'boring details' and then you are going to give me more info there too. [*Marks a place on the text.*] The way you can do that is on the other side here you can write number 1 'more info' and then number 2 'more info' then we can put it back in the story. OK.

When everything was finished my Dad left reminding us that on Monday our parents would pick us up at 11.00 to 11.45.

Oh. I see, it was a weekend camping trip. You were not missing school or anything. So there might be something to put in here. [*Indicates place in text.*] Are these real people? Julie, Carole, Jenny?

Holly   Yeah.

Johanna   They are friends of yours? So this is sort of what you would imagine if you had a trip with these girls. They are all good friends? OK.

That night we talked all night and really pigged out and slept most of the day. At around 3.00 we went for a bike ride and discovered two things. It gets dark fast, and even when there are really clear skies it can rain out of the blue.

OK. How did those two things affect you? It sounds as though you rode back in the dark soaking wet. Is that what happened? Can you write another sentence in there that will tell us what happened to you? It's hinted at but it's not clear that it actually happened to you.

For dinner we ended up eating chicken noodle soup and sandwiches, for desert chocolate donuts, Oreos, marshmallows, lots of jelly babies.

OK. This is the Friday night?

Holly   No, Saturday.

Johanna   Can we put that in here? [*Writes.*] More info here. It's hard for me to keep track of what day it is. So, if this is Sunday this is cute because traditionally Sunday dinner is an event, and this is your event.

So that night, forgetting our parents were coming at around 11.00 . . .

Johanna   Now, 11.00 could be that night, so you might want to make it 'the next morning', which would make it clearer.

That night, forgetting that our parents were coming in the morning, we pulled another all-nighter and the next day we were woken by our parents, not too pleased to see we were not ready to go or even dressed. So that was the end of our camping trip. It might not have been exciting but at least I know who Jenny likes.

You have told me about the eating but I don't know much about your friends. You wanted to go out and have fun, I know about that, but I want to know more about what happened at night, what you stayed up all night talking about. You pulled two all-nighters, that's a lot of talking. Do you not want to put that in the story?

Holly Yes, I think I'd like to put it in.

Johanna OK, where can we put it?

Holly Right here, after the first night.

Johanna 'We talked all night and really pigged out.' That's where you want to put what you talked about? Because this, finding out 'who Jenny likes', refers back to the conversations you had. You haven't told me anything about talking about boyfriends or whatever, so this refers back and sort of makes more sense to the reader. The problem with writing a story sometimes is that you know the story in your head, but the person reading it has somehow got to get that from you.

Holly Yeah, that's what I had to do, keep on going back and adding things.

Johanna This is a lot of work you did here. When did you do this?

Holly On Saturday. I had nothing else to do, so I worked on this.

Johanna Great stuff. So you are going to put more into here [*points*], number 2 is going to go in here, and number 3 is going to go in here. Number 4 is what happened, so you put that here. So you are going to write those pieces now, alrighty. This is going to be a great story.

(11 November, pp. 437–441)

* * *

The two episodes in this story show Johanna's repertoire in transition. The broad frame of the lessons reflects the practices I contributed to our collaboration – making space for teaching at the point of error – and the fine detail of the lessons reflects the generous and personal patterns of face-to-face interaction which characterize Johanna's teaching. In the first example, Johanna watched and listened to what was happening in my writing conferences.[3] The second example, a few days later, shows how she integrated what she saw me doing into her own practice. She did not merely copy what I was doing but transformed it with her own sense of how teachers should speak to students. Whereas my conference with Natalie focused on issues of writing craft – structure, plot, climax – Johanna's conference reflected her skill and commitment to dealing with students' feelings as well as their thinking. Johanna shared her enjoyment of reading Holly's story, asked her about her friends, praised her for the special effort she had made, reassured her that the additional effort she needed to make would result in 'a great story', and also gave her a series of pieces of craft advice concerning level of detail, chronology and communicating the writer's feelings about the events described. Despite my commitment to this kind of attention to the whole person, which surfaces in the strategies I use to deal with students who are too frightened to begin writing, I still had much to learn from Johanna about putting these ideas into practice.

While Johanna was integrating my way of teaching writing with her way of teaching children, she was also unknowingly learning to meet the writing goals of the current Intermediate English Curriculum Guideline (Ontario Ministry of Education, 1987). Had she originally sought the answer to her question, 'Do you think they learned anything?' by consulting the guideline she would have found that the process approach to writing was mandatory (p. 18) and teaching grammar and spelling in context were recommended (pp. 21, 22). What she would not have found was any practical advice about how these elements might be combined into a teachable programme, or how such a programme might be integrated into her own established repertoire.

Instead, through our collaboration, she had developed a practice consistent with the guideline. In the two Grade 7 classes this practice was already working well while the two of us were present. The problem, as Johanna mentioned to me at the end of the 11 November lesson, was how she could continue these writing lessons after I had gone. How would she find time to get right round the class and read students' stories? My experience was that there would be little trouble in finding time in the two small classes, and less trouble with the larger Group 3 class once they learned to work more quietly, energetically, and for longer without direct supervision. How that happened is the story told in the next section.

THIS IS RUBBISH

Despite Johanna's careful record-keeping, and despite having two teachers working with each class, some of the Grade 8 students in Group 3 had continued to fall behind in the producion of their books. This may have been a consequence of our decision to work with students on their texts in class rather than collect them to take home to correct, but it also seemed to be related to the generally low levels of energy and productivity we had managed to draw from the Grade 8 class. One of the strategies we thought of (7 November) was to make up a large chart which showed the name of every student in the school, listed vertically, and the individual steps in the book production, listed horizontally. We asked students to place ticks next to the steps they had completed, and thus were able to tell at a glance which students we might need to hurry along. This seemed to help, but we still had problems with Group 3. During Johanna's non-teaching time (9 November) we sat in the staffroom and discussed what else we might do with this large and intractable class.

Johanna	[We could] take out the work that is rubbish and say, 'This is rubbish, this is not Grade 8 work.' If I were to mark this right now I would have put more effort into it than Prentice did.
Bill	What's the best way of doing it? Is that going to . . .
Johanna	They know when they have done nothing.
Bill	Some of those students are beginning to drive me mad, like Geoffrey.
Johanna	But Geoffrey moans if he doesn't get exactly

> what he wants at the right moment, and then does nothing.
>
> *Bill*   Eldora has written something which is essentially juvenile . . .
>
> *Johanna*   So is Julia's.
>
> (9 November, p. 421)

Plainly we were both very irritated by the work which was – or was not – taking place in the Grade 8 class. As we talked, we decided to work down the class list and divide students into three groups: those whose work was up to grade level; those whose work was below grade level but who were working as well as they could, and those whose work was not good enough.

> *Johanna*   Richard?
>
> *Bill*   I don't know.
>
> *Johanna*   He has a terrible time with writing and needs learning centre help and the learning centre teacher hasn't come back to me. He's a mess. He can't work with distractions. I don't know what to do. Yelling at him is not going to help. He's a separate case. Julia?
>
> *Bill*   It would be hard to growl at her – she's done what we asked – but she could do better I would have thought. With students like her I would take partial responsibility myself. I haven't put the pressure on beforehand, she's been allowed to do the next four steps because she has done the task when others haven't. At some level, you lose the capacity to tell her it wasn't good enough.
>
> *Johanna*   So the story was not that great? She can make a better story by saving the pictures and working harder on the writing. In many cases there are fix-up things you can do. Martin, have you checked his?
>
> *Bill*   Yeah. It's scrappy junk but he did the task. I

wouldn't make him do it again, but he would
benefit from simply finishing the task instead
of doing whatever comes into his mind on the
day.

(9 November, pp. 423–4)

These discussions about individual students continued, and
Johanna began counting the number of students in each category.
There were just eight in the category of students whose writing was
up to standard. Johanna went on to discuss the changes she thought
we ought to make.

Johanna	One of the things that has been occurring to me more and more in that class is that we have got to start running silent classes. It's too distracting.
Bill	It's a pity, but it feels like that to me. The lessons have worked perfectly well in the two other classes. It's almost as if you need a different pedagogy. We are trying to teach in exactly the same way in the three different classes.
Johanna	I found that last year too. . . . OK, so what shall we do with this little list? Tomorrow, theoretically we have science but my suggestion is that we slog on, but only if they are actually doing something. It's ridiculous to keep wasting time.
Bill	OK, so here we have a strategy choice. One thing we could do is to split them. I could take a group into another room. The problem with that, I suppose, is that it doesn't get us any further forward towards the class working together. So what does it teach them: if they mess around enough we will take the problem from them and solve it for them.

Johanna	You are beginning to sound like me. [*Laughs.*] Sounds like a class meeting, Bill.
Bill	It's a river that flows both ways.

(9 November, pp. 424–6)

The next morning, we put this plan of action into effect in Group 3. Johanna began the Grade 8 lesson with a class discussion about the limited progress many of them were making with their stories. Before the lesson began, Johanna arranged the stools in a circle and as students came in she asked them to sit in the circle. Several students preferred not to, but Johanna insisted that they join the class meeting by physically joining the circle. Then she explained that we had talked about the class and agreed that there was a lack of commitment to learning:

> We divided the class up – in terms of writing and
> doing work – into students who were working at
> Grade 8 level, then we had a group that was working
> below Grade 8 level, and there was a group that was
> working below grade level for one reason or another
> and are going to bring it up. But there are others of
> you who are writing stories that are Grade 4, 5, 6
> stories. You know that writing such stories is laziness,
> lack of commitment, or a feeling that you don't need
> to do it. Basically, what we are getting from you is
> something that means you are going to fail writing. We
> had a whole group of students who did nothing
> last class, who used maybe 5% of the class time. . . .
> So what we want to do is to get suggestions from
> you about what we are going to do about this. Bill
> and I have some ideas about what we could do, but we
> want to hear from you.

(10 November, p. 431)

Instead of suggestions, the class began a series of complaints about unfairness, poor instructions from the teachers and so forth. From their point of view, there seemed to be no possibility that our dissatisfaction was well founded or that students might need to change their behaviour.

Martin	The first day we wrote the story Bill said, 'Write anything that came into your head', so if we are writing Grade 4 . . . we never knew that it was supposed to be a story.
Johanna	How many people have Martin's understanding of the assignment? [*Many students raised their hands, and Johanna asked Will to comment.*]
Will	If I had of known that it was important I could have written a much better story.
Johanna	Does anybody here have a different understanding, that this was actually going to become a story, a book?

(10 November, p. 432)

Several students said yes, but the weight of opinion was that the idea that the story would lead to a book came as a complete surprise. This was, of course, a rather wild notion. My field notes included a series of transcribed explanations from earlier lessons which contradict this widely shared feeling. Harnessing her incredulity, Johanna went on to attempt to unpick the history of the assignment, carefully reminding people of the steps we had taken from the first period of silent writing. After listening to a series of stories from students, Johanna attempted to play back what she heard people saying:

My feeling is that you feel as if there is some disconnection, that we have attacked you on your story writing and you are trying to defend it in terms of not knowing it needed to be so special. What Bill has been saying from the beginning was that what we wanted to get from you was a good story. In many of your cases you have gone completely away from the camping trip. We have got a million different stories now. The point that I am trying to make is that people are wasting class

time, the work that is happening in here is not at
Grade 8 standard for many people, and we have to solve
the problem. What you are trying to say, I think, is
that we never told you that we expected Grade 8
work.

(10 November, p. 433)

At this point seven or eight people were struggling to respond,
including Brian and Guy, who were desperate to find out whether they
were in the 'bad' group. I caught Johanna's eye.

Johanna   Yes, Bill.

Bill   What I hear quite a few people saying – just as
you have said – is that the instruction wasn't
clear and now they are being told it isn't Grade
8 work. They would have done better if they
had known it mattered. I don't know about
you, but I would be quite happy to
reconsider the whole task if that is what people
want.

Students   [*several people*] Oh, no!

Bill   Hold on, you can't have it both ways. I would
be prepared to start again with people, not to
do a book but to do the best Grade 8 story
they could. If individual people who have not
done well wanted to start again they could
write a new three-page story and not make a
book. There are people who are nearly finished
who would not want to do that, but the people
who are saying, 'I didn't know', would be better
to find a way of moving on instead of
saying . . .

Johanna   . . . who's at fault here.

Bill   . . . who's at fault and this is hopeless. We want
Grade 8 work from everybody.

(10 November, p. 433)

Johanna asked for comments on this suggestion, or for alternative suggestions. The comments concerned a plethora of issues: whether teachers could describe grade levels, whether there are some people who just can't learn to write well no matter how hard they try, whether the stories had to involve camping, whether the stories were for children or not. Johanna's response was not to reply to the comments people were making, but to attempt to move the discussion on.

Johanna	Guys, we are going to waste the rest of this period if what I am hearing now is excuses about why you are at the stage you are at now. We need to make a plan for where we are going to go from here. You know that Bill and I have both said that we are not happy with what you are doing. We feel that you can do better. There are a bunch of people we are happy with.
Lance	Johanna, if we come to you later can you name them?
Johanna	Yes, you can find out where you fall later. Now, the people who have not been doing their best work here are in the group that we are wanting to help. We want to help you make this the best story you have ever written. I have got to see a class where students are working hard. I don't want to see a class where students are spending their time socializing. This is a school. During class you work. Do you have any suggestions?
Julia	Can we just start? Can we just work?
Johanna	We can just work if you feel that is enough. Is there anybody who needs Bill or me to organize the class in any other way?
Brian	Two groups. We could put one outside and one in here.
Johanna	It's too many students in one room? One with Bill and one with me. OK.

After a whispered conversation with me, Johanna announced that we
would go with Brian's suggestion.

> Bill is willing to take the students who feel that for one
> reason or another they have not done a story they are
> proud of. He is willing to take those students, start
> again with them, and help them. How many students are
> in that position or would like to work with Bill? Hands
> up.
>
> (10 November, pp. 434–5)

Seven students volunteered, and so I took these people outside to work. First, I went into the open area, but quickly realized
that it was not appropriate. As one of the students said to me,
'We came out to find a *quiet* place to work.' Instead, we ended
up sitting or sprawling across the hallway floor outside Johanna's
room. This worked quite well. One by one, I got each of the students started and they all worked energetically until the lunch
break.

The next morning I continued to work in the hallway with this
small and lively group of boys. At the end of the lesson I took
Lawrence's story in to Johanna for her to read. It was neat, interesting, correct: a vast improvement on the writing he had previously
produced. Whether as a result of more personal attention, or the
decision they had taken to start again on their stories, these
students continued to work well. Johanna also reported that the
remainder of the class was far more productive in their absence. At
break on 11 November, we talked briefly about Group 3 in the
staffroom.

Johanna	Now how did you get Lawrence to write like that? The first story was abysmal.
Bill	I didn't do anything. I just said, 'Is this your best work?' He chose to do better, for some reason, sat on the floor of the hallway and wrote. He finished it today and read it aloud to me. I gave him no advice about it. I just said, 'That sounds really great', because it was. Like

Martin, he made some changes as he read through the story and noticed things that were not quite right. Then I said, 'Get some clean paper, use my pencil, and print your story really neatly so that you can be proud of what you have done.' With Martin – you know what an energetic kid he is – he had scratched madly and written a story last time about death and violence, and today he scratched madly and wrote another barely connected story about death and violence. Different character but just more death and violence. So then we had a conversation about cartoons and how he knew that one had come to an end. Then I said, 'So, does this one come to a proper end?' and he said, 'No, it's just two stories that aren't connected.' Then we talked about how he could get an end here . . .

Johanna   You're so smart.

Bill   . . . and then I suggested an end and he was most enthusiastic about that. Now I could genuinely praise the thing and I think that I can persuade him to write it out neatly, putting in direct speech and so on. Now, it's worth doing.

(11 November, pp. 443–4)

Inside Johanna's class there had also been some changes. With seven people absent, including most of the more fidgety boys, it was easier to establish a quiet and purposeful working atmosphere. There was even time for one of Johanna's 'learning from experience' conversations with a small group.

Johanna   Everyone worked quietly. . . . Lance came up to me and said: 'It's useless, I can't possibly work in class. I will have to do it at home.' I said, 'I want you to try.' He said, 'I'll just rip it up, I'll just throw it out', and I said, 'I just want you to try.' Karen came up in the meantime and said, 'I can't write like this.' I had told her I wanted her to take her story and set it at Community School. She said, 'I can't write like this, I just can't do it.' So I tied the two of them together and said, 'Richard and Adam have the same experience as you and Lance have about doing any writing at all, ever. At home, anywhere, it's hard work. You are both experiencing that level of frustration here in the room. I want you to go and experience it. It's hard, but go and do it.'

Bill   You were saying, 'I am not going to save you?'

Johanna   Yes, 'It's going to be hard, you are going to feel frustrated, but have to go through it.' So they went off and did it. So at the end Lance said, 'I wrote a page and a half, but you haven't seen it.'

(11 November, p. 445)

* * *

'This Is Rubbish' deals with a sequence of three related episodes: a problem-solving discussion in the staffroom; the class meeting; and the lesson which followed the decision made at the class meeting. The staffroom discussion began, like so many discussions among teachers, with an exasperated exchange about our students' deficiencies. They had made no 'effort', their work was 'juvenile' and was 'beginning to drive me mad'. Behind this exasperation was our unexpressed disappointment that we had not resolved the education–control dilemma as well with this class as we had with the two Grade 7 classes. We liked what we had achieved with those classes and when we couldn't establish the same busy working atmosphere with Grade 8 we blamed the students. Having allowed ourselves the brief luxury of moaning, we acknowledged that the problem was not all due to students' wilful misbehaviour. Some students had educational and emotional problems that were beyond our influence, and others had met our formal demands, if not our highest hopes for them. Notwithstanding these special cases, Johanna firmly expressed the opinion that the best solution to the problem was to insist on silence while students were writing. She felt that she could not allow the time-wasting and poor standards of work to continue.

My reaction to the suggestion that we insist on silence – 'What does it teach them?' – reflects a further development of our collaborative relationship. On the one hand, I knew that Johanna would normally prefer to negotiate with students than to assert her right as a teacher to make up the rules, and on the other hand Johanna knew that I normally had no objection to insisting on silence while students were writing. Johanna was amused to realize that I was reflecting back her own best intentions at a time when she had temporarily lost contact with them. Instead of following my more blunt and pragmatic instincts, I recognized that Group 3 might learn something positive about being independent if they took part in some classroom problem-solving. When I used the expression 'the river that flows both ways',[4] I was alluding to the mutual learning that this discussion represents for us both. Not only was she learning more about the craft of teaching writing, as I knew it, but I was learning new ways of helping students to take responsibility for their own learning.

When we met the class the next day, Johanna had not lost her irritation about standards of work. She was particularly clear about what she saw as 'laziness' and 'lack of commitment'. Johanna and I were both surprised at the students' reactions, and unwilling to accept their version of events. So, although Johanna followed her usual pattern in class discussions of summarizing what she understood students to have said, she also insisted that they attend to her definition of the problem: 'people are wasting class time'. Despite students' insistence that they had not known this story mattered, Johanna reminded them that 'this is school' and what that means is that during class 'you work'.

This insistence may be seen as a limiting case of Johanna's range of acceptable resolutions to the education–control dilemma. She believes that students should not arbitrarily be controlled for the teacher's convenience, and that they can learn from participating in decision-making, but that in the end the relationship between students and teachers is not symmetrical. Just as she rejects the practice of 'independent time' in the open area, she rejects the notion that students' and teachers' opinions about education are of equal value. She is determined to change the situation in Group 3, enters the class meeting with that in mind, and continues until Brian makes the suggestion which she and I had canvassed the previous day in the staffroom.

In the third section of 'This Is Rubbish' we reached a more satisfying resolution of the dilemma. The absence of the small group of boys who sat with me in the hallway meant that Johanna was able to improve the working tone of the rest of the class without being arbitrary or punitive, and my close personal attention to the more needy group in the hall meant that they, too, were able to meet our standards for quality and effort. Within this firm framework of control, Johanna could once again proceed with her agenda of helping students learn to be responsible for their learning. Her characteristic response to the few students who could not write in the newly quiet environment was to show them that there were others who had the same problem, to describe the problem in terms of feelings, and insist that they could best overcome the feeling of frustration by being more persistent. Here, on a smaller scale, she was able to help people learn from their experience. On the larger scale of the working atmosphere of the whole class, however, she was not willing to endure weeks' or months' more frustration in the hope that students would learn to work independently and energetically in a group of 30. Instead she provided a structure which limited their options, was clear about her own requirements, and continued to help students to learn from their experience on a safe and achievable scale.

FINISHING UP

In the last few weeks of the illustrated book project our teaching was uniformly pleasant and rewarding, and we could see some return for our struggles with Group 3. The small group of restless students I taught in the hallway mostly made good progress and their absence made it much easier for Johanna to keep the rest of Group 3 on the straight and narrow. My work with the small group followed the familiar pattern of students reading their stories out aloud to me, correcting the errors together, and discussing my craft suggestions.

On 18 November an artist employed in the school board's artists-in-schools programme visited Community School to show students how to make hard covers for their books. The procedure was complex and Johanna told me that it took three explanations before she was confident she understood the process, so she expected that there would be some students who would need help. She had made three large charts full of detailed instructions, and for the next few days we used these to help students make their impressive and professional-looking hard-covered books.

We continued with the book project into the dying days of the term. On 24 November, for example, I cut up some standard covers for Johanna, so we were able to spend most of the lessons helping students to lay out their book covers or to cut covers for the non-standard-sized books. These lessons passed very pleasantly, with Johanna and I both busy helping happy and enthusiastic students do a sensible practical activity. On 30 November we spent another three delightful hours working together with her classes on proofing the final texts, illustrating the books and constructing the hardback covers. The students were now so involved in this project that the classes were a dream to teach: lively, light, productive. All three classes went very smoothly without any explicit preparation by Johanna or me, or the use of force to keep students to their tasks. They were now spread out across different stages of this long and interesting activity and we had plenty of time to pay attention to individual students who needed it.

On 30 November Johanna spoke to the whole class for no more than three minutes during each of the lessons, and gave a mini-lesson to six or eight students who were ready to learn how to make their hard covers. At the morning break, after teaching Groups 1 and 2, I said to Johanna, 'These are the classes I always dreamed of working with.' She agreed with me about how much fun the classes were, but said that she was not convinced that the book project had been worth the time and trouble. Next time, she said, she would make the project much shorter. But when the Group 3 lesson went equally well – fidgety Guy and Brian working with real energy, for example – Johanna told me that she had changed her mind. Despite the drain on time of this larger than intended project, it was all worth while.

* * *

During this final part of the book project, Johanna and I sat in her room during one lunch hour and talked about her reaction to the writing classes we had been doing together.

Bill Can you give me a summary of where you think we are up to with writing?

Johanna OK. I have learned a series of skills to do with helping students to write. I have added to my repertoire now. What we have done I would be able to do again, to refine it and get students to produce a story.

Bill Are there particular things that you remember picking up?

Johanna Oh, you want a list? OK. First of all, to provide quiet in-class time. I have a whole variety of starting points from you. One is to let them free-associate. Another is to give them one of your stock story starters: the time they almost died, the time they were really scared, the inside of the purse. Another thing is the steps you use in proof-reading: having the friend read it and tick off the best bits; having someone read it for spelling, having them go home and fill out the best bits; ways of filling out; ways of speaking to students about their writing. I think probably I need to go over the notes for a lot more of your language because you've got things that you say to students that I need to memorize.

Bill Things that you hear and think, 'That worked?'

Johanna Yes. With Group 3 I have learned the lesson of

setting higher standards for them and letting them know that they are not meeting my expectations.

Bill   It came as a shock to me how simple it was to improve the quality of the stories. It was shocking that it was as simple as saying, 'It's not good enough.'

Johanna   Yes. [Laughs.] That's always the old argument in teaching. At what point does, 'It's not good enough' become discouraging? It's still a fine line but I am less ... I think we stumbled on the way to say it. It's much more devastating when it's said personally to one kid. We said it to a whole class. We said, 'Most of you are not good enough.' I think that helped us.

(21 November, pp. 462–3)

As Johanna says, our resolution to the education–control dilemma with Group 3 treads 'a fine line'. With the two Grade 7 classes we were able to establish a working environment which satisfied our sense of what was educationally defensible without requiring us to exert very much explicit control on the students. The interest of the task, the detailed assistance we had time to offer, and their enthusiasm for learning was enough incentive for the Grade 7s to produce polished and professional illustrated books. With the more demanding people in Group 3, the resolution was different. We found that we needed to be more explicit about what was and was not acceptable, and to work more closely with the most reluctant and needy students. Once we did so, the Grade 8 class became as easy to work with as the Grade 7 classes had been all along.

Unlike the apparent finality of the resolution fixed here in text, teachers' real-world resolutions are less permanent. Resolutions, like generalizations, decay. In the time beyond this study, Johanna would probably continue to struggle with the dilemma of how much control she was willing to exert over Group 3 and which of her educational goals she was willing to sacrifice. The fine line of her resolution would depend on a series of influences outside Johanna's direct control: how often students arrived late from break or the open area; how much the experience of the book project changed students' expectations about writing; how much more serious the Grade 8s became as the spectre of high school closed in on them; and how Johanna managed this new pattern of teaching when she was the only teacher in the classroom.

SUMMARY AND CONCLUSIONS

Neither Johanna nor I began the school year with any intention of teaching an extended series of writing lessons. We stumbled into teaching writing because Johanna was dissatisfied with the quality of some student writing she had planned to use as text for the illustrated book project in art. Together, we tried to find a better way of helping students than handing out dummy punctuation exercises for correction. These concluding remarks will touch on two issues from this series of lessons: the relationship of repertoire to the problems thrown up by a subject area new to Johanna; and the further development of our collaboration in these lessons.

Two issues may be distinguished in the analysis of the relationship between Johanna's repertoire and her experience of teaching writing in the illustrated book project. One, the most readily dealt with, was that she tried to assimilate some of my craft knowledge into her established patterns of teaching. She asked me to describe what I would do instead of teaching sentence analysis, took notes on what she saw me doing and, faced by new problems, asked me to show her what I would do. The more difficult issue was to find a comfortable resolution to the version of the education–control dilemma thrown up by the pattern of teaching writing I brought with me. The particular resolutions Johanna and I reached in the lessons described in this chapter were among the many possible resolutions we might have considered or stumbled upon as we taught these three classes. From these stories I want to draw attention to two characteristics of the resolutions we reached: they were context specific and biographical appropriate.

The control problems we faced with all three classes flowed directly from educational decisions we made, and from the problems inherent in my preferred pattern of teaching. Because I believed that the most useful thing I could do with students was to talk to them one-to-one or in small groups about the problems they had encountered in their writing, I encouraged Johanna to allow each class to spread over various stages of writing the text for their illustrated books. One of the consequences of this pattern was that the writing part of the project took more time than we had expected. Johanna was, after all, responsible for these students' art, not their writing. Faced by this problem we decided to draw up some charts with the various steps in the book project marked on it, so that we could more closely monitor progress. This tactic was enough to solve the problem in the two Grade 7 classes but made no difference in the Grade 8 class. This led, in time, to the crisis described in 'This Is Rubbish'. Following the class discussion, a clearer statement of our expectations, and the brief period of working in two separate groups, we resolved the problem of productivity with the Grade 8s. This class required a different resolution to the education–control dilemma posed by the patterns of teaching I brought to our collaboration, but the final resolution was as satisfactory as the easier resolution we achieved in the Grade 7 classes. By the end of the project, there was little difference in tone between the three classes. They were, as I said to Johanna, the classes I had always dreamed of teaching.

Such resolutions, however, are unstable and reflect the particular context in which we were working. In classroom work the teacher's imperative is to act, to respond to what is happening at the moment and then to move on. This action always involves some resolution of the education–control dilemma: in 'This Is Rubbish' we provided a tightly controlled environment that ensured that appropriate standards of quality and productivity were recovered before people proceeded with their artwork. Resolutions such as these are unstable and could have been upset by any one of a host of actions taken by teachers or students, or by forces outside the classes. Judgements about the quality of each temporary resolution to the education–control dilemma depend, among other things, on the specifics of the context. Different resolutions would have been required by other teachers, if we had been teaching another subject, or if there had been just one teacher working with three classes of 30 students.

The second point to be made about these resolutions to the dilemma is that they were shaped by the predispositions to action which we carried forward from our previous experience of teaching

105

and by our biographies. This point may perhaps be made more crisply by introducing a term drawn from the work of Hans-Georg Gadamer, the philosopher whose epistemology underpins this study. Describing the process by which the understanding we bring from the past is tested in encounters with the present and forms the understanding we take into the future, Gadamer (1975, p. 273) uses the term *fusion of horizons*:[5]

> The horizon of the present is continually being formed, in that we have continually to test all of our prejudices. An important part of this testing is the encounter with the past and the understanding of the tradition from which we come. . . . In a tradition [the] process of fusion is continually going on, for there the old and the new continually grow together to make something of living value without either being explicitly distinguished from the other.

Transposing Gadamer's terms from the hermeneutic understanding of written texts he had in mind to the understanding of action which is my concern, we may see the *horizon* as the predisposition to act in certain ways in the classroom. Johanna's predisposition to act, I have argued, is shaped by her understanding of her own biography, and by the patterns, content and resolutions to the education–control dilemma which together make up her repertoire. The fusion of horizons, then, is the imperceptible growth and change of the horizons of understanding she draws forward from the past, through the present and into the future.[6]

To return to the particular actions I am concerned to understand, and to make this argument more concrete, my insistence on silence while students were writing in 'Do You Think They Learned Anything?' was part of the horizon I brought with me to Johanna's classroom. It grew out of my own journey from a *laissez-faire* introduction to teaching, through my survival years, and through my interest in the craft of teaching writing. In the well-practised introductory lesson I revived from my repertoire in 'Do You Think They Learned Anything?', I was unconcerned about using my authority to insist on silence while people were writing. I explained this to myself and to Johanna in terms of the educational value of helping students overcome their own resistance to writing and fear of judgement. Another consequence of this pattern of teaching was that my awareness of the problem of control disappeared. The lesson met both my theoretical and practical requirements and, like Johanna, I might have said: 'I have learned how to do a [writing] lesson that works.' So for me insisting on silence, being clear about standards and splitting the class in 'This Is Rubbish' involved no change in my horizons. The change in my understanding was that I became more concerned about the consequences of such arbitrary actions for the students' progress towards independence. Working with Johanna had helped me understand more about this issue and so when Johanna was overtaken by disappointment and inclined to go with my blunter instincts, I reminded her that we might follow one of her patterns of teaching and discuss the issue with the class.

For Johanna, one of the key tests of an appropriate resolution with the Grade 8 class was that we found a way to help them be more productive without discouraging students. In a comment already cited, Johanna had talked about the consequences of discouragement for her own confidence when she was learning to play the clarinet. Also, about the time we were wondering how best to deal with the lack of productivity in the Grade 8 class, she told me a story about an unsettling conversation with a parent at curriculum night. The parent's criticism had been unfair, she thought, but she supported his right to complain when he thought that his daughter was being discouraged at school.

> *Johanna* What he thought she was going to learn was
> discouragement. . . . I don't think she was
> discouraged. He's absolutely right if he is
> coming in to tell me, 'Don't discourage my kid.'
> I am in [to see the teacher] like a flash when I
> feel my kid is being discouraged.

> (7 November, p. 409)

The issue of discouragement, she went on to say, was related to the central unresolved issue at Community School: how students learned to become independent:

> It's the whole crux of the issue of Community School. At
> what level can you let them go? You cannot let them

become discouraged, to give them time to waste. They can't handle it. [One way was to] let them fail miserably and let them suffer the consequences and then realize that they would have to pull their socks up. My feeling about that was that it was such a discouraging experience that it made them angry and they ended up doing it for the teacher, not for themselves.

I think with Group 3 we are going to have to give them a lot more help. With most of those kids last year the only thing that really helped them was a personal conversation telling them what they had to do. Last year, whenever I had a project due I would write up all the steps. They couldn't read it if I handed it out.

(7 November, p. 411)

We did give them ' a lot more help' to complete their work, in a way that would not involve individual discouragement, and which used one of Johanna's well-practised patterns of teaching. At bottom, she was prepared to insist that 'this is school' and this means 'you work', but it was important to her that the message was not delivered in a discouraging manner. Fortunately, we found a way to say it that was reasonably comfortable for her. For other teachers, of course, our resolutions to the education–control dilemma would not seem as satisfactory. It is not hard, for example, to imagine teachers who might bring different horizons of understanding to problems such as we faced, and who might either find my insistence on silence while students were composing unconscionably arbitrary, or my postponement of concern for spelling and grammar an abrogation of teachers' responsibilities for standards.

The major conclusions of this chapter concern the almost imperceptible changes in Johanna's repertoire which I have characterized as fusion of horizons. While these changes in her understanding of teaching were taking place, our collaborative relationship also changed. Unlike the lessons described in 'Repertoire', where my role was as an observer and helper in Johanna's classroom, this chapter has shown the two of us working together more collaboratively. Johanna was still in charge, but inside and outside the classroom we worked as a team, discussing what we had done and consulting each other about what we would do next. Johanna continued to make most of the announcements and management decisions, but we were working inside the larger framework of my preferred pattern of teaching writing and as the lessons proceeded I rediscovered teaching skills and patterns I thought I had forgotten. By the end of the illustrated book project most of the students seemed to be enjoying the programme that Johanna and I had developed and we both considered what was happening to be educationally worth while.

Besides the fun we had, this change in role gave me access to a kind of data I had not expected. Now that I had begun teaching, I had access to observations about changes in my own understanding, in addition to my observations and reconstructions of Johanna's teaching. A second consequence of joining Johanna as a colleague relates to my ethical stance in the study. When Johanna was in the process of deciding whether or not to participate in the study she talked several times about the risk of having the 'mistakes' she made recorded for posterity. I attempted to protect her from this risk in several ways: by the provisions for anonymity and confidentiality; by giving her the right to veto any particular word or phrase in the text; and by making a commitment to including her interpretations alongside my own should they differ substantially. None of these provisions, however, could protect her from awareness that I was watching her work and recording it in my field notes. Nor could they protect her from the shock of reading hundreds of pages of detailed notes, descriptions and arguments about her work. Few people outside public life ever face the kind of scrutiny that participation in a study such as this entails. My work in her classroom, however, provided Johanna with a day-to-day reminder that 'making mistakes' was not just a characteristic of her work or mine, but a characteristic of all teachers' work. In teaching, nobody ever gets it completely right.

NOTES

1. See Chapter 4 for an extended treatment of this and other science lessons.
2. Berlack and Berlack (1981, pp. 135–65) have used the term 'dilemma' to describe philosophical tensions teachers face. My use of the term follows Lampert (1984) and Olson (1985), both of whom

speak of dilemmas in terms of the practical problems which must be resolved by teachers in action.

3. The notion of writing conferences and my pattern of teaching writing more generally is drawn from the work of Graves (1983).

4. A reference to the opening words of Margaret Laurence's *The Diviners* (1974).

5. The term *horizon* had previously been used in the philosophy of Nietzsche and Husserl to describe the finite understanding available to a person at a point in space and time.

6. There is more to be said about the influence of *tradition* when, in Chapter 6, Johanna's teaching is considered in the context of research on teaching more generally.

Chapter 4

Science

Not all changes in teaching are as successful and satisfying as those described in 'Writing'. Sometimes teachers are asked to teach subjects for which they are not well prepared. This chapter describes one such case, the experience Johanna and I had in trying to find a comfortable way to teach science, a subject which was unfamiliar at the beginning and still mysterious to us both at the end of our collaboration. Our first attempt at overcoming the mystery, described in 'Breaking Glassware', was to teach from the school board's set of standard lesson plans. Johanna appreciated the effort I made but, as she said in 'Spitting Wooden Nickels', she thought we would be better off working with students' interests than with content which seemed so abstract and inaccessible. Consequently, we changed our approach, developed an independent research assignment, and then helped students through it in lessons such as those described in 'Wheel of Fortune'. This account of our experience in teaching science ends with 'Going Native', a story in which our collaborative relationship turns full circle, leaving me immersed in the action of teaching and Johanna asking what our action has to teach us about the possibility of students' independent learning in schools.

Johanna inherited responsibility for Community School's science programme as a result of the reduction in staff from four teachers in 1987–8 to three teachers in 1988–9. Consequently, the remaining teachers had to divide up the subjects previously taught by Bob, the teacher who moved on to another school. For the most part, this involved people teaching a little more of subjects they already knew, but for Johanna it meant taking on a whole new subject area. Creatively, she decided to combine her need to learn to teach science with my offer to help out in any way I could, and ask me to take some initiative in teaching science. This was not an area of strength for me but, undaunted, we began to plan for Grade 7 and 8 science in the new school year. Our first step (30 June 1988) was to arrange a visit to another science teacher Johanna knew.

When we arrived, our colleague showed us the way he taught science, through an individualized science programme. He had a filing cabinet full of folders for each of the lessons and extension activities he wanted students to experience in two years of senior school science. When our colleague realized that Johanna had never taught science before, he cautioned us against such an individualized programme. He mentioned that he had a long history in teaching science, and had taught science in the conventional way for many years before he began building up his current individualized programme. He had first begun with more class-centred lessons, using the school board material, and suggested that we should also do that. He recommended that we talk to the consultant, get the school board books, and borrow some of their equipment.

As we drove away from his school Johanna wondered aloud about the value of the programme we had been shown. She thought that some of the people she knew who taught science in alternative schools would see more emphasis on content than process in this programme, and she could not see how this would help students grasp the key process issues in science, such as the scientific method. On the other hand, she acknowledged that when she had seen science taught by a discovery approach some students seemed to discover no more than how much time they had on their hands. When she asked me what I thought we should do about our programme for next year, I suggested that we take our colleague's advice and begin with a fairly straightforward whole-class-oriented programme. Later, I thought, we might be able to build up to a more individualized approach.

TEACHING THE SYLLABUS

The formal science programme began (on 4 October) after students returned from the camping trip, and a week before Johanna and I began the lessons described in Chapter 3. In the days before I began teaching science we decided to use the standard introductory unit, 'The Nature of Science', for the Grade 7 classes and the unit called

'Solutions' for the Grade 8 class. The afternoon before the first lesson, I collected and washed all of the school's science glassware and found substitute materials for the chemicals mentioned in the school board's intermediate science syllabus.[1] That evening I planned an introductory lesson on solutions for the Grade 8s. I wanted a lesson which would be interesting, would convince them that I was a real science teacher, and would not require me to lecture or them to make notes. So I decided on a version of the first lesson in the syllabus, a practical activity involving lots of coloured liquids and glass. My lesson plan had six steps and included word-for-word preparation of the instructions I intended to give about the experiment. As I said to Johanna the day before the lesson, the possibility of mess and breakage might be a good thing because it would give me a genuine reason to assert the need for order during science classes.

Breaking Glassware

As always, Group 3 drifted into the room, late and rowdy. Johanna's first comment to the class was that they were wasting time. She explained that I was going to take the science lesson today, and went on to warn people that they would be using equipment that was breakable and supplies that were messy, so those things would only be available to people who were in control of themselves. She also made a number of housekeeping points: homework, the afternoon's excursion to the art gallery, and the agenda for the student meeting later in the day. When she handed over to me, I began with essentially the same points about equipment and behaviour:

> OK, before we start I just want to ... [*pause to wait for silence.*] Before we start I want to say again what Johanna has said. On the bench over there are about a hundred pieces of glass, all of which are breakable, which we are now going to proceed to fill with a series of liquids, all of which will stain your clothes. And in the middle of that we are going to be carrying half-buckets of water across the classroom. Consequently, it is essential that you actually do the tasks in the order I say, and attempt to not pour the liquids on each other.

Another way of saying that is that there are two ways of teaching science. There is the way I was taught science at school, which was, 'Take out your notebook, turn to page 57 in the textbook and copy down the four characteristics of a solution.' The way I would rather do it is by doing experiments.

(4 October, pp. 231–2)

I explained that I had organized some experiments for today, and reminded students – again – that the liquids could stain, the water could spill and the glass could break. My sermon complete, I moved on to a brief class discussion intended to introduce the term 'solutions'.

Bill	Does anyone know what a solution is?
Geoffrey	An answer.
Bill	Yes, that's one possibility, what's another?
Prentice	A mixture.
Bill	OK, a solution is a mixture, a special kind of a mixture. Does anyone know what sort of a mixture it is?
Julia	A whole bunch of different things mixed together.
Bill	Yes, it is a couple of things mixed together. Yes, Will?
Will	It's a liquid.
Bill	Yes, it's often a liquid. What else?

(4 October, p. 232)

There were no further suggestions forthcoming, so I moved on to explain that the next few lessons would help the class understand the differences between a mixture and a solution. The first experiment would be to make up some mixtures – poster paint and water, sugar and water, coffee and water, chocolate and water and oil and water – and then work out which ones were that 'special kind of mixture' we call a solution. Then I divided the class into groups and asked one person from each group to collect a bucket from me and to half fill it with water. Immediately, the class began chattering and I insisted on silence while they waited for the next instruction. As soon as the first group had their water ready I began issuing the rest of the equipment: graduated cylinders, conical flasks, measuring spoons and so on. The atmosphere was busy, but noisy, and I began to worry that things were going to come unravelled. Johanna, perhaps sensing the same thing, put aside her marking and asked what she could do to help. She helped me to hand out the materials and equipment for a few minutes, until I was ready to give the rest of the instructions:

Bill	Stop. [*Claps hands.*] Listen in please!
Elsa	He said, 'Stop listening.'
Bill	Stop and listen [*very carefully articulated*]. I will just try that once more: stop and listen please. [*Finally, the class settles and listens.*] Now, what we are going to do is make up five mixtures of things, so you are going to come and get each of the five mixtures from this end of the table. Then, you need to follow the instructions written on this blackboard.

(4 October, p. 233)

I read out the instructions I had written on the blackboard before the class, asked people to draw up a chart for their results, and helped people to get the materials. As before, they listened reasonably well while I was explaining what to do and demonstrated how to mix the substances, and then broke into light chatter as they waited for the equipment and materials to arrive at each bench. Johanna and I were busy helping each group to get organized and answering their questions. Several minutes into this process, I heard the crash of glass breaking on the floor. I turned to the area where the noise had come from and spoke very forcefully to Bea, the girl who had dropped the conical flask:

115

Right. Just stop! [*The class turned to dead silence for the first time.*] There are essentially two problems with what happened then. One is it shows me that it is going to be hard to do this kind of science, and that is a general and ongoing problem that I am worried about. The second is that this group no longer has a container to mix in. I guess I can solve the second problem by finding another container, but *I* can't solve the problem of you doing things which causes you to break glassware. Only *you* can solve that problem. Are we on the same wavelength? Can you find a broom and clean up, while I solve the second problem. *You* solve the first problem.

(4 October, p. 234)

I was secretly thrilled at the opportunity this breakage had offered. As I responded, I sensed that I was able to make the point I had begun the lesson with, without preaching as much as I had before. The class was subdued for some time and I returned to the task of answering questions and explaining to individual groups what to do. Did the water go in first? How much water? Which water should be used? Notwithstanding my careful instructions, it was necessary to repeat them for several groups. By this time in the lesson, however, it was possible to be fairly businesslike: many groups knew what to do and the rest were keen to get the experiment right. For the next 20 minutes Johanna and I were busy answering questions as each group worked through the five mixtures I had prepared for the class. At one point, I realized that not many groups had been filling in their charts, so I called the class to order. Just marginally, this required less effort than the previous time I had asked the class to listen to me.

Bill   The last substance is oil. I want you to make sure that you don't do the oil until you have done the rest, as it will be hard to get the oil residue out of the bottle when you have finished. As soon as you have the five substances, you need to fill in the chart. So if you would just watch my hand [*indicating the chart on the board*]. You will actually have to turn around in order to look at the board. Even people who are pouring things. Good, this is almost right. [*Expressing satisfaction at the level of attention given by the class.*] Even Lawrence is beginning to turn this way. OK, so you have got to . . .

Johanna   Eldora, look at Bill, watch the board.

Bill   I cannot guarantee that this will be a wonderful aesthetic experience – looking at me – but you *will* understand the task.

(4 October, pp. 234–5)

I talked through the chart in detail, with the sense that everyone was taking in what I was saying. Johanna, however, called several students to order and asked several questions intended to clarify what I was saying. By now I felt much looser about teaching than I had, and the class seemed to be working on this complex and untidy task reasonably well. The lesson time drew to a close before all of the students were ready, so we all hurried to fill in the chart of results in time. As usual, Johanna had table captains dismiss their groups and waited at the door to check whether people had been dismissed correctly. As Brian and Guy left the room I congratulated them on working purposefully and getting through to the end of the experiment and I asked them if I could keep their work as a sample to show the class next time we met.

* * *

This lesson, my first-ever science lesson and the first lesson of any kind I had carefully planned for many years, was a very rich experience for me. In the commentary which follows I will explore three issues: my reflections on the lesson the evening after I taught it; what I noticed in my new role as a teacher *and* a researcher on teaching; and the first of many discussions between Johanna and I about the purposes of our science programme.

117

To begin with my own reaction to the lesson at the time, my field notes show that I was very pleased with what had transpired, chiefly because my control goals were achieved. With a little help from Bea, I had managed to carry 26 students through a logistically complex and reasonably orderly science lesson. Whatever the students might have learned, I considered the lesson a success because students had taken it seriously. It had not been easy, I was still struggling at the end of the lesson, but I had survived without humiliation. Beside this achievement, students' learning about science in this lesson was relatively unimportant to me. I knew that some of the decisions I had made in the class did not advance the cause of understanding the characteristics of solutions, but quickly forgave myself. I had, for example, abandoned my plan to begin with a little lecture on solutions when it seemed more important to begin with the activity I hoped would capture their interest. Nor did the brief question-and-answer session I conducted instead seem to have been particularly helpful in introducing the ideas.

I may have quickly forgiven myself my imperfections, but Johanna had some serious reservations about the impact of the lesson. She mentioned after the lesson that she had noticed that only about half of the students were listening to my careful instructions on filling in the summary chart I had drawn on the blackboard. The rest seemed to expect that someone would explain what to do later. Although I was not aware of this at the time, I was not particularly concerned when it was pointed out to me afterwards. Compared with the disasters I had imagined in the days leading up to the lesson, it seemed very successful. The class seemed to have had fun, I had needed to give fewer reminders about behaviour as the lesson continued, and I had begun to establish myself as a teacher as well as a researcher in the school.

In this lesson I had attempted to take on the metaphorical white coat of scientific certainty. With no more knowledge of solutions than my half-remembered Grade 12 chemistry and what I had read in the syllabus, I was presuming to be authoritative about the characteristics of solutions: there really were six unambiguous characteristics and I could name them. When I had finished teaching the topic, I would expect the students to be able to do the same. I made no attempt to link this knowledge to their experience, and indeed had insufficient background to generate reasons why it might matter that they knew the difference between a mixture and a solution. What I was attempting to teach was 'school science', the science in the syllabus and the science I have seen taught by science teachers around me in high schools. This was not the kind of science education which appears in the first few pages of science guidelines – not the scientific method or the spirit of enquiry – but the science embodied in the details of lesson plans from the recipe books circulated by the school board.

Whether or not what I had done was educationally useful, the lesson had reminded me of several things about knowledge and reflection. I realized that this version of science teaching posed quite different problems of organization and control than those I was used to resolving in English. I could not teach this kind of science, even badly, without more careful lesson preparation than I have come to regard as normal in English. Those test-tubes, the five different coloured solutions and the buckets of water inevitably take longer to prepare than an idea for a story to write or a photocopy of a poem to discuss. I also had to think more carefully about exactly how every group would collect the equipment and materials, dispose of the excess liquids and tabulate their conclusions; if people made the oil and water mixture first, for example, they would need an additional trip to the classroom's one sink to wash the flask. No matter how familiar this lesson plan and these organizational problems might become with experience, someone would still have to collect the materials and glassware, carry them into the room and later return them to their storage place. One of the consequences of my lesson preparation in this case, and perhaps more generally in science, was that my investment of time in preparation made me more than usually committed to following the lesson plan I laid out in advance. It also meant that I was locked into my estimated time allocation for each part of the lesson if I was not going to have equipment left out at the end. So, notwithstanding my inexperience as a teacher of science, this lesson made me wonder whether science lessons such as these would work against the possibility of spontaneity that I have come to take for granted in the teaching of English.

My reaction to the broken conical flask is an example of the kind of consciousness I had about the actions I was taking. In the planning stage I had welcomed the logistic complexity of the lesson and the possibility of breakage as it would provide me with a legitimate reason to insist on more order than the Grade 8 class had been accustomed to. My experience as a teacher had taught me that lectures on the consequences of inappropriate behaviour are far less effective than examples. I did not know in advance what the context for an example would be, but expected that this lesson – fraught with opportunities to spill, stain or break things – would provide one. I had done all of this thinking beforehand and made some of it explicit to Johanna in a discussion the day before the lesson. Then I taught the lesson without any conscious awareness that I was waiting for something to be broken. Indeed I was trying to organize things so that nothing should be broken. But when Bea broke the conical flask I quickly turned the event into an example of what happens when students are restless during science experiments. This was not an old trick, in the sense that I was conscious of having used it before, but it did come from my history in that I knew that a practical example would be more useful than any amount of hectoring. I was not consciously waiting for the opportunity provided by the broken flask, nor did I have time to see it as an example of a class of events I had been waiting for. It all happened more quickly than that: I heard a crash, I reacted, and I heard myself making explicit a connection between the event and the general rule that I had anticipated might come up at some time during the lesson.

The third issue this lesson raised was the relationship between this version of science and Johanna's notion of a useful science programme. She had already expressed reservations about two kinds of science teaching. She was doubtful about the uncontrolled 'discovery' science lessons she had seen lead many students to waste their time, and had wondered whether the individualized approach used by the science teacher we visited might lead to an emphasis on content rather than the more important process issues. The day after the 'Breaking Glassware' lesson we talked at lunch about the goals of science and she mentioned that the lesson on solutions had not seemed very useful to her, either. I suggested that the goal displacement in my science lesson was probably not unusual in intermediate science teaching.

Bill   On one level [science] is about setting up
        problems, hypotheses, observing, inferring and

so forth. . . . On another level there is 'school
science', which is about using a beam balance,
knowing what a solution is, carrying around
a rack of test tubes without breaking
them . . .

Johanna That's the science I am not the least bit
interested in. . . . I think there are so many
interesting things that it is worth researching. I
think one of the things we should do in science
is set a term project for the kids, and that
they work on it at home, do their own
research.

(5 October, pp. 256–7)

Johanna suggested that we make more use of independent research
projects in science. We spoke about the possibility of splitting the
programme between independent research and more of my school
science from the syllabus, but neither of us was satisfied with this
compromise.

Johanna Can't we do one of the topics as a research
topic?

Bill Probably. The school actually has a lot of
science books. They are in boxes and we'd have
to pull them out and look at them. We could do
Tuesdays as taught science and Thursdays as
either independent field trips or research. We'd
have to look and see what material we had
in the books. It wouldn't have to be what's
in the curriculum. . . . So, shall we do a
50/50 split between school science and real
science?

Johanna At the least. I sort of thought we might be able
to make it all real. We can't, eh?

Bill We could, but it's hard work. It's hard enough
work for me to decode the book and work out
the lessons. With the Grade 8s I am really

121

> pleased to have a highly structured thing to run
> on, because the more steps there are the less
> chance there is to lose control.
>
> (5 October, p. 259)

Johanna remained unconvinced of the educational value of my plan to continue teaching science from the book, but I was reluctant to leave the security of the syllabus. I taught several more science lessons, some of which are described in Chapter 7, before we discussed this issue again.

Spitting Wooden Nickels

The week after our science programme began, Johanna had a discussion with the school board's science consultant, and afterwards called me to talk about our science programme (16 October). Her discussion with the science consultant had left her with the feeling that the main role of intermediate science was to get students interested in the subject. The consultant had said that all of the content would be covered again in high school. Johanna's feeling was that the standard materials we had been using seemed unlikely to promote students' interest in science, so we ought to explore some other approaches.

When we talked more about our options a few days later (18 October) Johanna explained that what she was looking for was something that was going to be 'fun for the kids and not a lot of work for us'. The problem, however, was that neither of us had sufficient background in science to teach it as well as we would have liked, whatever approach we used. I argued that in view of my ignorance, the easiest approach would be to continue following the book.

Bill	I feel like the easiest thing would be carefully prepared but quite stupid lessons about the six qualities of a solution because at least I can go to the book. I can't extemporize in science.
Johanna	Do you know what I am tempted to do? A science teacher I was talking to said that one of

the things kids are really interested in is
biology of themselves and comparing this with
the biology of animals. OK, so what we are
going to do is get into biology which makes
much more sense. We'll just tidy up what we've
done on the nature of science and solutions,
recover as much self-respect as we can, and go
on to human biology.

Bill This is all terrific and I endorse your
enthusiasm, but I know more about chemistry
than I do biology, and you've seen how much I
know about chemistry!

(18 October, p. 312)

Plainly, we were at cross purposes here. I was reluctant
to leave the safety and security of the published materials, and
Johanna was reluctant to waste students' time with pointless
'school science'. She was not sure what our next step ought to be,
but had a clearer image of what a good science lesson would be
like.

Johanna I know what I want to do, I know what I
want it to look like, what I want to have
happen. I want to have a class where the
kids are paying as much attention as they
were [in a recent nutrition class Johanna had
taught]. They were all asking questions about
these diseases that either killed their relatives
or thought might kill them. I want them to
want the information that they have to
look for. So that they are actually doing
scientific research and learning about science
because it is something that concerns
them. Boy, they are really interested in
health. They are interested in the ways their
bodies work and they are interested in sex,
so it seems that we could do that and call
that biology and no one's going to complain.

123

> But, how to actually have it happen day to day
> is tricky.
>
> (18 October, p. 313)

Johanna suggested that science for the rest of the term should be based on a long biology assignment dealing with the sort of health and disease issues which we knew interested our students. They could work in pairs on different topics and then make a presentation to the class at the end of the term. I volunteered to have a look among the school's science books for material we could direct students to, but I must have done so with less than my usual enthusiasm:

Johanna   You sound really tentative about this. What about it won't work?

Bill   There's a clash for me between your image of what a good class would be like and . . .

Johanna   What we know of these kids?

Bill   When you describe to me your image of what the class would be like, I think, 'Yup, provided we had the materials organized the 7s could do that and might learn a lot from it', certainly as much as if we gave them notes and exercises. But it just sounds like a logistic nightmare with those 8s.

Johanna   [*Laughing gently*] I'll prove you wrong.

(18 October, p. 313)

After lunch I sorted through the science books for appropriate resources for Johanna's biology project. Although there was much less specialist material on human biology than I thought we would need, there were several sets of textbooks. That evening I wrote a draft assignment which I thought might be closer to Johanna's idea of a useful science programme, and which could be supported by the books we had on hand. Selecting the relatively broad topic of 'Living Things', the draft assignment asked students to describe the growth of a plant, to classify some leaves, to describe the life cycle of an animal, and to plan and write up an experiment. Some of the assignment could be completed at home, and other parts would require some assistance from us at school.

At lunch the next day we talked again about what to do with science. I expressed some concern about departing from the guidelines. I was, after all, going to write about these lessons and wanted to check that Johanna was willing to make them public.

Johanna   Let me tell you what I think about guidelines. I would argue this with the area superintendent, with anyone. They can attack me and pillory me, I don't mind. As I know it, the spirit behind the guidelines, as stated by my science consultant, is that students will be better able to deal with the science courses that they are required to take at high school if they have had some sort of introduction to science in Grades 7 and 8. The intent of the guidelines is to give them a sampling of different fields in a way that is going to excite them.

(18 October, p. 324)

Since the purpose of the senior school science programme was to excite students' interest not to ensure that they mastered specific content, it seemed to Johanna that we ought to attend to their genuine interests. There was no relevance to their lives or ours of the kinds of information I had been pursuing in the work on solutions. In the long run, she thought, teaching to their interests would be more useful and easier for us to do.

Johanna   So to teach science you have to find out what they are really interested in, what they would be willing to do. You can even try and make them interested in solutions, and you can stand on your head and spit wooden nickels – which is basically what we have been doing – and bamboozle them into being interested in

> solutions. Or, you can do less work, or the same
> amount of work, with something that really
> gets them going.
>
> (18 October, p. 324)

After an interruption while Johanna helped resolve a problem between a student and an itinerant music teacher (described in 'Conferences'), I inadvertently cut short this discussion by producing the draft assignment I had prepared. She liked the assignment because it centred on some of the essential ideas in the 'Classifying Living Things' topic in the syllabus but used a process that seemed more congenial to her. We moved on quickly to discuss whether we had the books to support the assignment, and I showed her the material I had organized the previous day. We decided to move it all into her room. After we had finished organizing the books, and while I prepared a final formal science lesson for the Grade 8s, Johanna cleaned up the art room. She cleared all of the benches, restacked art materials and washed down the sink. At the end she stood back and admired our work, saying: 'There, *that's* better!' We were now ready to teach the kind of science programme she could believe in.

* * *

This short series of discussions marks two important turning points in the science programme Johanna and I shared. The first is that Johanna relinquished the role she had begun to establish in science, as an observer and helper, in much the same way I had been helping out in the lessons in Chapter 4. Until this point our roles had been symmetrical. She would take the lead in planning and teaching art and music lessons and I would help out and later talk to her about what she had done. In science she had begun by playing a symmetrical role, leaving me to take the lead in planning and teaching while she helped out in the classroom and afterwards discussed the lessons with me. In 'Breaking Glassware', for example, she was on the periphery, helping by writing on the board or answering questions. After these discussions, and the writing lessons which began a few days earlier (13 October), we both left behind our observer roles and had begun to team-teach much more collaboratively.

The second turning point in these discussions concerns the direction of the science programme. Despite my reactionary attempts to keep the task simple by following the book, this approach seemed more difficult and less educationally defensible to Johanna. We disagreed and, as I had come to expect, Johanna provocatively asked me 'What did they learn?' after each lesson.

> **Bill** I can see you at every turn, like I am pushing to teach science straight, to follow the bloody book [*Johanna laughs in recognition*] you find a reason why we can't. You always like it when I teach those science lessons to the Grade 7s because I do it lightly, the kids gather around the bench and it becomes an activity lesson. As soon as I try to do it with twenty-six it becomes a school lesson and at the end of it you make some disparaging remark – in the politest possible way!
>
> (25 October, p. 348)

Johanna laughed, again, and I guessed that she would be much more comfortable if we taught science with a pattern of teaching more like her art teaching: limited teacher directions at the beginning of the lesson, most of the time given over to activities, more emphasis on the larger goals and less on the content objectives of the syllabus, and more time for issues of genuine concern to Johanna and her students.

As Johanna's ready acceptance of the assignment I had planned indicated, such a programme was much closer to her own sense of educationally defensible teaching. And for myself? I was not deeply concerned about the outcome of our discussions. My primary concern was not with the teaching itself. My interest was in working with Johanna in order to learn about her understanding teaching and how it changed, and these discussions were helping me do that, whatever the outcome for the science programme. My second concern was that I wanted to save Johanna part of the effort of preparing and teaching

127

this unfamiliar subject, as a way of returning some of the time and effort she had contributed to my work. I knew that I could make a contribution whatever style of lessons we adopted. Finally, having checked that she was not concerned about the fine detail of the syllabus, I was happy enough to move on to a more relevant and less technical kind of science. Although I had enjoyed bamboozling us all with science and would have been willing to continue, I recognized that this 'spitting wooden nickels' was not educationally defensible by my own standards, either.

LIVING THINGS

Once we changed to a pattern of teaching which was more compatible with our separate ways of teaching and closer to the pattern which was developing in the illustrated book project, science became much easier for us both to teach. Johanna began the next section of our work in science by introducing the assignment to the Grade 7 and 8 classes (25 October). In each case, she handed out the science assignment first, talked through the questions, and reminded students that if they were going to grow a plant they should begin that day. In the next set of lessons (27 October) we helped students sort through the science books in search of suitable experiments to perform as part of the assignment. Generally, I sat at the table in front of our stock of science books and Johanna moved around the room. Many students had questions and possible experiments they wanted to discuss, and others wanted help using the index, the tables of contents and layout of the science books to locate experiments. After a few of these lessons Johanna and I decided (1 November) that it might be helpful if we had a series of lessons which showed students how to complete each of the five tasks on the assignment. The two stories that follow include two lessons intended to show students how to write up their experiments for the assignment, and a lesson which gave students an opportunity to locate a suitable experiment.

Wheel of Fortune

The demonstration I used to explain how students ought to write up their experiments was one I had prepared but not used during the abandoned unit of work on solutions. I planned this lesson (1 November) as a demonstration and accompanied it with a handout for students to refer to later. I had given no thought to how I might manage the lesson until the Grade 8 class began filing into the room. Then it occurred to me that the experiment could be done in the format of a television game show, a format I had practised as an English teacher. It may have been the after-effect of Hallowe'en chocolate on their energy levels, but the Grade 8 class required some careful settling down. Johanna reminded students that they should sit in their allocated seats, and then moved several students who were still too close to their friends for our comfort. Just before we started, Johanna looked across the room and said, 'Will you start?' I took this question to mean, 'Which one of us gets the job of settling down this squirrelly bunch?' I began in the time-honoured way, asking the class to 'Shh', and then speaking to a couple of students about their behaviour. In this case, I asked two boys to put the Hallowe'en sweets they were chewing in the bin. Then I reminded the class that one of the questions in their science assignment asked them to conduct an experiment, and explained that Johanna and I had thought that they might like some help in planning and describing their experiments. I asked them to read the handout I was passing round and announced that I was going to talk them through another example of an experiment while they took notes. Their reaction was less than instantaneous, so after about 30 seconds I raised my voice – not in anger, but over the background babble – and reminded the class that I had asked them to read and said that this should be done in silence. This had some effect, and so I was able to circle round the class and help the more reluctant individuals to begin reading.

Once they had all started, I collected three stools and placed them on the rug in the centre of the room. On the left-hand stool I put a large graduated cylinder of tap water and a beaker of table sugar, and on the right-hand stool I put a mixture of poster paint and tap water. On the middle stool, I put two conical flasks and in each conical flask I put a glass funnel and filter paper. When I finished setting up, and while students were still reading, I whispered to Johanna: 'What we'll do is get them to write down the experiment I am going to do and then we can check it before they go' (1 November, p. 371).

As soon as they had all read through the handout I asked people to take out a piece of paper and write 'Problem', the first of the four headings on my handout, at the top. Still sheep-dogging the class,

I found several students some fresh paper and lent one the pencil I habitually wear behind my right ear while I am teaching. Finally, ready to begin, I introduced the lesson:

> The first task in setting up a science experiment is describing the problem. What is it you don't understand? What is it you want to find out? What is it you expect to show? On the sheet, I have described the problem of distinguishing between a solution and a mixture. When you do your experiment in the 'Living things' project you will need to come up with a problem statement which starts with a question, 'Why . . . ?' or 'What . . . ?' or 'How come . . . ?' That's your problem statement. The experiment we are going to do here is another one on solutions. I am going to want you to write down a problem statement something like this. . . . Oh, just a reminder before we start. Johanna and I want you to have a good example of how to write up an experiment, so we are going to check your notes before you leave. OK. The problem here is, 'Does the solid filter out of a solution?' You could just write that down. You know when you make a solution you put a solid and a liquid together, so, does the solid filter out of a liquid solution?

> (1 November, pp. 371–2)

Several times I repeated the notes I had dictated. Next I asked students to make a second heading, 'Method'. There were cries of 'Wait, wait', and 'What's the problem again?' I rushed on, trying to force the pace so that the whole class would have to attend. When some students needed to ask Johanna what I had dictated, I offered to write it on the board. I looked at Johanna – who seemed to know why I was rushing on – and when she shook her head I continued my break-neck dictation. When I was ready to go on to fill in the method section I asked, 'Who wants to be Vanna White?' There were lots of offers to play the part of this hostess from the game show *Wheel of Fortune*. I chose Bea, but as I did so I happened to catch Mark's eye and noticed that he seemed disappointed so I invited him to be the male Vanna White. While Bea and Mark came into the middle of the room and stood behind the stools, there was a series of cross-talk about male and female hostesses and game shows, which I quickly brought to a close. Raising my voice above it I said:

> Right! Leaving aside Vanna White for a moment, in the method section of the experiment you need to write down exactly what happened. What I am going to do is get you to write down the exact steps we take. What we are going to do now is to filter two different mixtures of a solid and a liquid. So, Vanna, will you take 15 mls of sugar and put it in the graduated cylinder?

(1 November, p. 373)

Bea poured the sugar into the graduated cylinder and added a litre of water, while I dictated, in three or four different forms, a description of what she had done. I then gave the graduated cylinder to Mark and asked him to shake it and try to dissolve the sugar in the water. After a little shaking there was still some solid at the bottom of the cylinder. I asked him to let me have a try and then shook it vigorously, like a cocktail shaker. At this point one of the students began to sing, 'Shake it, shake it, shake it.' Perhaps I did it theatrically, because the response my shaking drew was, 'Oh wow. What skill. Now do it one hand', and so on. Next, one of the Vannas poured some of the mixture down the filter while I dictated. As soon as people had caught up with the dictation, we moved on to the next step.

Bill   Step number 4. A mixture of 15 mls of poster paint and 900 mls of water was poured . . .

As Mark poured it, several students asked whether the mixture was shaken, and I explained that I had shaken it very vigorously before they had come into the room. By now, everyone was following the little bit of theatre in the centre of the room and making notes as I dictated them and Johanna and I repeated them. Mark and Bea, especially, were primping, spinning around and smiling wildly at the audience in their Vanna White impressions. Mark, who never seemed quite sure that he could play a female character, kept up a whispered conversation with me about the cross-dressing $M*A*S*H$ television character, Corporal Klinger.

I went on carefully to describe the observations, drawing from the two Vannas that the sugar-water was clear, transparent and contained no floating solids, whereas the paint was cloudy, blue, translucent and contained floating solids. Secondly, my student assistants described the differences between the filtrates and the condition of the filter papers, walking around the room to demonstrate what they had observed. Most of the blue paint solids were filtered out of the paint mixture and the filtrate was clear, transparent and a very light blue.

Finally, I dictated the brief conclusion that, based on their previous work on the characteristics of a solution, the sugar-water was a solution but that paint was a mechanical mixture. I then briefly explained to the class that in science new experiments were built on the experiments and theories of the past. In the 'Living Things' assignments, the conclusions of their experiments might well include references to supporting theories or evidence they might find in science textbooks. We ended with a brief round of applause for my assistants, and then students were asked to show Johanna or me their notes before they left the room. Everyone seemed to have made a reasonable effort. As Mark, who had taken his role very seriously, walked away from me he said, 'That's the closest I've ever been to Pat Sajak.'

* * *

This story shows how Johanna and I approached our new goal for science teaching: helping students to organize their own learning in science through the assignments. With this Grade 8 class, it was difficult to achieve both of these goals simultaneously. Much of our effort went into harnessing their enthusiasm, which we did at some cost to our educational goals.

Although I had decided on the spur of the moment to use a game-show format for the demonstration, the characteristically spirited entry of Group 3 meant that the class was not at first ready for a game. Instead, Johanna and I began a round of ritual settling down activities. We moved several students, asked others to put aside their sweets, and I briefly raised my voice. There was no sense of desperation in the exercise of this control. We were quietly doing what the students expected us to do at the beginning of a class. Having brought the class to a state of unstable equilibrium, we could begin the lesson but were still not ready for the game. I asked students to make their own notes as I carried out the demonstration and told them that we would check their notes before allowing each student to leave for lunch. Although I had momentarily forgotten that the class already had my prepared notes in front of them, I knew that this would keep them busy and quiet during the demonstration. To make sure, I found the stragglers some pencils and paper, and I began dictating so fast that people had to struggle to keep up with me. Once I achieved sufficient equilibrium in the class, it was possible to introduce the instability of the game show without the class collapsing into chaos. From then on, the combination of the theatre taking place on the rug in the centre of the room and the relentless pressure of the dictated notes kept students interested and busy.

At the end of the lesson Johanna told me that she had enjoyed it. Eldora, one of the more serious and mature girls in the class, had also said to her, 'I like it when we have science. We learn things but it is fun.' Despite these two votes of approval, and my own enjoyment and satisfaction at teaching it, the lesson was a limited success. Judged by our goals, we made some progress towards teaching the scientific method. We had shown students how to organize their assignments, but we had made no progress towards the larger goal of helping them learn to work independently on topics they were interested in researching. Despite Johanna's warning about 'spitting wooden nickels', the difficulty of keeping the class busy and productive had led me back to a similar pedagogical place. In this case, instead of bamboozling them with science I had distracted them with a game show. By recycling a piece of English teacher's repertoire I had turned a potentially difficult encounter and a potentially boring dictation and demonstration lesson into a piece of theatre. It could have been worse – I could have bullied and bored them – but the lesson was controlled and artificial compared with the best of the writing lessons we had taught. Like the television show on which it was patterned, the surface glitter and pace disguised the lack of substance.

Going Native

A few days later (3 November) the Grade 8s were back to their intractable best and I was thrown back to struggling for control. In this
lesson, I made my final step in the transition from researcher to
teacher at Community School.

The class straggled into the room and I began by counting heads.
Only 18 of the usual 28 had appeared. The rest, it transpired, had been
excused for other school activities but those who did appear brought
with them the crazy feeling that I had noticed during the morning
meeting. Miles, who usually managed the morning meeting, had been
away from school, Johanna was not well, she and Freida had both been
irritated by students' behaviour and had told them so, and the meeting had run 5 minutes over time. I looked at Johanna and asked her
whether I should start, and when she nodded I began the class. My
first attempt was a failure, so I raised my voice and insisted on
attention.

> Listen in, please. Let me try again, what you have to do
> this period . . . [*Waits.*] What you will have noticed in the
> school today is that Miles is away, Johanna is still sick,
> Freida is feeling pretty low, everyone is working hard
> trying to organize curriculum night, and things are
> coming a bit unravelled. So that's an example . . .
> [*Impatiently*] Come on! Listen in please! So, we have a
> science lesson which I would rather teach going
> downstream with you, not swimming upstream against
> you.
>
> (3 November, p. 389)

At this point, in a moment, the class tone changed palpably. I
made eye contact with Guy – an influential and fidgety student whom
I had learned to take as a touchstone of the class mood – and I heard
him say, 'OK'. The challenge the class had offered when first they
entered the room had melted away. Without interrupting the flow of
what I was saying, I was then able to change direction and go on to
explain the task. They were to continue work on their science assignments and those who had not yet found an experiment were to do so
this period. I explained that the lesson we had planned was one of

those which allowed people to work independently but which could easily decline into chaos:

> The trouble with working like that, which allows some of you to do this and some of you to do that, is that it has a way of getting unravelled. Just put your hand up if you know what to do next. Do you have in your mind what to do next in your science assignment? More than half of us, good.

(3 November, p. 390)

I then went around the class asking those who had their hands up to tell me what they were going to do next. Satisfied that enough were able to proceed, I asked Johanna if she thought we could deal with the rest of the class and then gave the class a final reminder about where they could find the materials they might need:

> It sounds like at least half of you are well on the way. If those people could just get started Johanna and I will help those who are not ready yet. Is that OK? Do people know what to do? I hope we don't come unravelled this period.

(3 November, p. 390)

With that, Johanna and I plunged into 20 minutes of finding and explaining experiments with a series of individuals or small groups. This was both useful and enjoyable. In a small group of students who need to know something, there was no need to insist on attention beyond that which I could legitimately command by my presence in the conversation. I was teaching the way I most liked to teach, with most people settled to work on a small part of a larger task they understood while I worked with a small group of students who needed some help.

After about 20 minutes, things did become unravelled. While I had been focusing on the small group I was talking to, the level of noise in the class had gradually increased. Concerned, I looked up in time to see a paper plane land on the floor. I seized on this and spoke very forcefully.

Bill	Right! Stop! The person who threw the paper plane go and get it. [*Geoffrey stood up and began walking across the room.*] That is the first step. I am going to count the people who I have noticed are working hard. [*I counted six.*] I may be misjudging some people but no more than half of the people are doing what they said they would do at the beginning of the lesson. The ones who have done it, that is good. That is what this school is about, working out what you have to do next and getting on with it on your own. The rest of you, I am not so pleased. Get with it!
Johanna	Bill, could I . . .
Bill	Some people, including Geoffrey who threw that paper plane, I spent about twenty minutes with last science lesson working through an experiment. I stopped what I was doing and helped you. Now, I find you throwing paper planes while I am trying to do the same job for three other people. It strikes me personally as unfair. How are we going to get this science going if I spend half the lesson explaining to one person and the next half of the lesson collecting his paper planes? This is not how education happens.
Johanna	[*to me*] Bill, what if they work silently? [*To class*] OK, the only people you need to talk to are Bill or me.

(3 November, pp. 391–2)

We then went back to what we were doing and the lesson played itself out very pleasantly. I was able to continue talking about experiments to Guy, Lawrence, Martin, George and Brian – in short to the group of boys who led the disruptive behaviour in this class. In a small group, however, they were interested in what I was saying and seemed keen to carry out the experiments we were choosing. We sorted through the experiments in the three science texts. Those I suggested included documenting human growth by using the height marks on the kitchen door-frame; capillary action in plants; using cellophane bags on plants to compare moisture in geraniums with and without leaves; demonstrating the process of osmosis using coloured liquids and Cellophane; and using a microscope to describe the structure of several kinds of cell. By the end of the lesson I was left talking to George alone. All the rest had chosen an experiment and moved off to begin their planning. As we walked out to lunch I was talking to a student about his progress with the science assignment and I said: 'This is good.' Hearing this personal formula of praise for progress, Johanna turned to me and said, 'I like it when I hear you say that, I know things have been going well.'

* * *

This story, 'Going Native', marks a significant change in my experience at Community School. It was ten months since I first began visiting the school, two months since I had begun attending four or five days a week, and a month since I had begun taking an active lead in teaching. In all this time I had deliberately maintained some distance from the teacher's role. I was in the school but not of it, participating in school activities but continuing to monitor my behaviour very closely. In this lesson I found that I had surrendered my observer status entirely. When I spoke to the class about my need to swim downstream with them not upstream against them, I did so as a member of the school community. When, half-way through the lesson, my appeal to the community spirit of the school began to decay I acted as if I had a right to invoke the school ethos, and a right to be angry with people who violated my sense of the school's goals and values. I paid no attention to Johanna's reaction to my outburst, and even spoke over her the first time she tried to suggest that it might be best to impose a rule of silence. In 'Going Native' I was no longer trying to 'pass' as a teacher at the school while I observed Johanna: I was now part of the school.

There is more evidence of this final submission in our lunchtime conversation that day. Miles, Johanna and I were sitting together round the staff room table and I was rehearsing my experience with Group 3, trying to understand it.

> Bill   The moment I said, 'Johanna's sick, Miles is
>   away . . .' I got about thirty seconds into that
>   and Guy said, 'Oh, OK', and I could feel a real
>   change come over the class. It was as if they
>   were thinking, 'He's got a good point there, we
>   don't have to go upstream.'
>
> Johanna   It was nice.
>
> Bill   I could feel it in the air that talking to them
>   straight was working. They don't get that much
>   preaching. So when someone says, 'Listen guys,
>   this is what is happening here . . .' they
>   respond.
>
> (3 November, p. 393)

Here, like every teacher who ever told a war story in the staffroom, I was trying to understand a surprising experience. I had not intended to appeal to the ethos of the school, and I certainly had not intended to speak so angrily to Geoffrey, but it had seemed to work. For most of the lesson the class managed to overcome the mood which was threatening to overtake the school that day. Somehow, what I had done had worked, a good lesson had emerged from the ashes of a terrible one, and I was still struggling to understand it.

A second consequence of the lesson was that this conversation precipitated one of Johanna's few challenges to the longer-term staff's version of the traditions of the school. Instead of joining me in these war stories, she was trying to draw more general conclusions from the lesson. She turned to Miles and said:

> It is so hard for them to work independently. I can't
> imagine that you guys ever did what you claim to have

done all of those years. Just watching Group 3 struggling
to work independently when there are two of us
supervising. There must have been eighteen kids in that
class at any time, but it was hard.

(3 November, p. 393)

This was a quite fundamental challenge to the history of the school.
Worried by the difficulty we were still having with the Grade 8s –
even with two teachers and a reduced-size class – Johanna had begun
to wonder whether they had ever had any success in teaching students
to work independently. Miles acknowledged that they had not always
been successful, and that dividing the school into those who could
work independently and those who needed supervision had sometimes
been necessary. He also suggested that at times it had helped to
'build the workload up a bit'. At present, he thought, students did not
seem to be under much pressure. This drew from Johanna a second
challenge to the school's history. Johanna's reaction (and mine)
was that it was not that they did not have enough work to
do but that they had too much free time and too little skill in
using it.

Johanna I've got so much stuff . . .

Bill Johanna's got them under quite a lot of
pressure. They have a whole stack of stuff to
do.

Miles They have been saying that, but that's good.
Then we can talk about budgeting time. But
I'm not seeing the Grade 8s behaving generally
as if they are under a lot of pressure.

Johanna I think that indicates the level of their ability
to use free time. I don't think that giving them
more free time is the way to help them to do
that. I think that they have got to develop
the skill, to learn how to do it in those
classes, because we are beating them over
the head.

(3 November, pp. 393–4)

139

Johanna had long been concerned about 'independent time', but I had rarely seen her suggest – even obliquely – that the other teachers should reduce the amount of free time students had, much less contest its value.

We were still a week away from the crisis in the book project (see 'This Is Rubbish'), where independence was the major issue, but in science the crisis had now passed and the remainder of our collaborative science teaching was completed without incident. In the weeks before the science assignments were due, Johanna and I continued to teach a series of lessons designed to help students complete each of their five tasks. We explained why biologists classify plants and animals, what was meant by the 'life cycle' of an animal, how to describe the characteristics of a living thing, and so on, rather than deal with the content recommended in the syllabus. A few days before the assignment was due, Johanna and I decided to provide a different kind of help. Concerned that we might find that some students had not made enough progress to submit an assignment, we spent a day (22 November) checking which students had completed which questions. To those who had not completed questions we gave fresh copies of the handouts we had been circulating with each of the previous lessons. In the case of the experiment, the largest and most important task, we went one step further and provided a set of simple photocopied instructions for the experiment.

As I walked into the school on the day the assignment was due (24 November) several students rushed up to me to say that they had their science assignments done. Prentice wanted a hug for completing his work; Rae hadn't finished, but still wanted to be in on the hugs. Lennie, who had made no progress as far as I was aware in the four weeks he had to work on the assignment, was sitting by the window looking through a microscope at a single-celled animal and called me over to share his enthusiasm. When I had been doubtful about replacing the safety of school science with the relevance and independence of Johanna's research projects, Johanna had threatened, 'I'll prove you wrong!' Judging by these students' reactions, at least, she had been right.

SUMMARY AND CONCLUSIONS

When this study was planned and negotiated, I gave Johanna's request for help in teaching science little thought. I knew how limited my background was in the subject, but approached the task as a practical way of helping repay Johanna for the time and effort she had committed by agreeing to collaborate in the study. Had she asked me to build her a set of bookshelves, or supervise the lunch room, or grade students' assignments I would have been equally willing to help out. How hard could it be, I thought, to teach a couple of hours' science a week to 13-year-olds? Consequently, I was surprised to discover how difficult it was to find a comfortable way of teaching science and how much our collaborative work in science contributed to my emerging horizons of understanding about teaching. Precisely because neither of us was sure what we could or should be doing in science, we had to be explicit with each other about our intentions and to spend some time comparing our impressions of the classes we taught.

The lessons in these stories about science overlapped those already described in 'Writing', beginning and ending a few days earlier than the writing lessons. I have chosen to describe these lessons after those in 'Writing', because it better suits the argument about teachers' knowledge that I have been constructing. In 'Repertoire', I described some practised and polished gems of Johanna's teaching, lessons where she acted so deftly that the education–control dilemma was submerged beneath the obviousness of her patterns of teaching. In 'Writing', I described Johanna's accommodation of my patterns for teaching writing. Together we struggled with the issue of students' independence which we had both brought unresolved to these lessons, and through the experience of team-teaching extended our individual horizons of understanding what it means to teach. Johanna added my pattern of teaching at the point of error and some craft knowledge to her established ways of teaching art; I had the opportunity to learn more from Johanna about attending to the state of students' feelings as I worked with them on their written texts. In the science lessons in this chapter we were both more obviously scrambling to connect the new subject to our established patterns of teaching, the content we already knew, and our customary resolutions to the education–control dilemma.

When first I began teaching science from the syllabus, I was surprised to realize how large an impact the preparation of demonstrations and experiments made to my patterns of teaching. Used to the limited physical preparation of English teaching, and in the absence of equipment which could be damaged or dangerous, I had learned to expect that I could trust my instincts and spontaneity as lessons developed. In science, however, I found that the commitment I had made to physical preparation and the need to have all of the equipment packed away by the end of the lesson led me to follow my lesson plans much more carefully. In part, this was no doubt related to my inexperience as a science teacher, but it was more than that. When I spoke to several colleagues who had been high-school science teachers I realized that the tradition of using experiments in science was a powerful force in shaping patterns of teaching. When I mentioned the incident in 'Breaking Glassware', both of the people I spoke to told me stories about limiting danger and damage to equipment in science laboratories. One colleague went further to say that 'for many teachers this becomes the purpose of the lessons itself: getting equipment out, used and replaced without chaos' (4 October, pp. 247–8). Whereas before I began teaching what I have called 'school science' I thought of this as goal displacement, I now realized that it reflected very real problems of management for which I would have to develop new patterns of teaching. Had I continued to teach from the syllabus – for some time – I presume that it would eventually have been possible for these control problems to be submerged inside a pattern of teaching consistent with my horizons of understanding about teaching, as Johanna had learned to do with analogous problems in teaching whole classes to play the guitar.

Instead, we decided to attempt to fit the new content of science inside our existing patterns of teaching. When we did this, we each contributed something to the task from our existing patterns of teaching. I often used those teacher-centred demonstration lessons, such as the game-show format of 'Wheel of Fortune', a pattern I carried forward from my more theatrical years as an English teacher. Similarly, Johanna contributed the pattern of independent research assignments which I had seen her use in a series of health and nutrition lessons (not described here). By using familiar patterns we were able to submerge our control problems of an unfamiliar subject. I no longer had to prepare step-by-step lesson plans to ensure that students would not break or spill things during experiments. Instead, as in 'Wheel of Fortune', I controlled the demonstration of the lesson and carefully balanced the stabilizing and destabilizing factors in the lesson but was never in any danger that the lesson would collapse.

Whatever patterns of teaching we may have had to choose from as we attempted to convert the unfamiliar into the familiar, we began our work in science with a very limited content knowledge base. I found myself in the position Johanna had been in when she planned her first writing lesson, in 'Do You Think They Learned Anything?' I had no useful experience of teaching the subject, so I had to draw on the more distant experience of what I had learned at high school. This, I found, was not very different from the content of the school board lesson plans so I presumed I could bluff my way through it. For Johanna, this was not really possible. She felt 'at a tremendous disadvantage' with the content of science and thus preferred to limit her teaching to material she found familiar. As she said at one point:

> I feel myself at a tremendous disadvantage when the kids
> ask anything. I think that there are little areas of
> learning in science that we could concentrate on and if at
> the end of the year they only understood what an
> experiment did that would be a valid year of science.
> That's a tremendously complex thing to know. I would be
> happy just doing little experiments with them all year.

(7 November, p. 407)

Had we felt more comfortable with the content, our assignment might have led us to teach more from the syllabus, perhaps the differences between the leaves of trees commonly found in Ontario and the stages of development of a frog, for example. Instead we directed students to the books we had collected, or asked them to locate this information for themselves. For Johanna, the problem with teaching the science of the syllabus is more fundamental than the gap in her content knowledge or her preference for independent research. More than this, she really doesn't believe that the content is very important. All around her she hears people give quite different and apparently scientifically based advice on matters she is interested in, such as health and nutrition. Knowing how to decide between the competing views seems to her to be much more important than knowing, say, the six characteristics of solutions. Besides, she and the students are already interested in choosing between the conflicting types of health advice they receive. As Johanna says,

> I looked deep into my heart and I couldn't find much scientific information. However I did find a tremendous interest in the adequacy of research. In nutrition I am getting them ready to make their own decisions about who they are going to trust. . . . I want them to be critical, to be suspicious, and to do their own research and make their own minds up. Then it becomes necessary to have knowledge. It becomes relevant if it affects your life.

(19 October, p. 325)

Although we maintained some distance from the content of the syllabus for most of the time we taught science together, we began our science programme with the syllabus and we needed the help of school science textbooks at the end of the assignments. In the final weeks of the work on the 'Living Things' assignment, having given students the opportunity and some assistance in working independently, we found that there were a still a few who seemed not to have found any experiment at all. Rather than allow students to become discouraged by failing the assignment we then chose to help them with a small piece of quintessential school science: a set of instructions for the very simple experiment on the stem structure of plants.

Throughout our science programme, Johanna and I faced a series of education–control dilemmas. Whereas I was pleased with the first few science lessons because they met my control requirements, Johanna had reservations about their educational value. From the first time we talked about the prospect of teaching science she had expressed doubts about the number of students who would benefit from 'discovery science', and she was doubtful about the content-centredness of the individualized science programme we had been shown. My school science lessons appealed no more than either of these, as she explained in 'Spitting Wooden Nickels'. Instead of trying so hard to make the connection between the syllabus and the students, her preference was to allow students to work with content that they already found relevant and allow them to conduct their own research. When she suggested that we use assignments to be completed at home, one of her established patterns of teaching, I had both educational and control reservations about her plan. Would they be able to find the appropriate material, I wondered, and would the Grade 8 class be sufficiently independent to complete such an assignment? She acknowledged that it would be 'tricky' to control but thought that the assignment I prepared had more merit than continuing to 'bamboozle them into being interested'.

Johanna and I did not always agree about the resolution of particular education–control dilemmas. In the case of 'Wheel of Fortune', for example, Johanna enjoyed the lesson and thought it a success, but I thought that the educational content was relatively thin. In part this reflects the connection between the lesson and my own personal interests. Just as Johanna was enthusiastic about lessons which might help people make decisions about which research they ought to trust, I was interested in lessons which explored the relationship between theory and a body of evidence.

When our science lessons ended, I was still unsure about whether they had been a success. The control problems had disappeared, but the educational value of what we had done was still unclear to me. Johanna had threatened to 'prove me wrong', but I was not sure that she had. When I marked the assignments I realized that they had been completed reasonably well. A few of the most able and interested students produced convincing and authentically scientific work. Most people followed the tasks we had set and taught but learned little more than they already knew about such issues as classification, life cycles and experiments. At the worst, they managed to turn the assignment into school science, by photocopying pictures of cats' life cycles from encyclopaedias. At the morning break in the staffroom that day, I mentioned that not many people seemed to have learned much. Freida was quick to contradict me. Her son Lennie, who attends the school and had called me over to look at his single-celled animal on the day the assignment was due, had got a lot from the work he had done. She was right in that case, I thought. Lennie had been fascinated by what he had learned and had written much more than I had come to expect from him.

With these concluding comments, the descriptive part of this study draws to a close. In Chapters 1 and 2, I introduced the case study teacher and her school, and argued that the knowledge embodied in Johanna's repertoire of teaching – her familiar patterns, content and resolutions to dilemmas of education and control – may usefully be conceptualized as 'horizons of understanding'. These horizons are almost imperceptibly reshaped as she encounters and overcomes each new gap in her understanding of teaching. In Chapter 3, where the gaps in understanding she encountered in the illustrated book project were relatively small, Johanna was able easily to add new patterns of teaching to her repertoire. These patterns, based on a view of writing teaching which I had previously used, were consistent with her hopes and dreams for education. The new content knowledge she needed to teach writing was consistent with the craft knowledge she already had about art and music, and was readily available from me. And furthermore, the practice of making time for writing conferences with students allowed Johanna to find a new context for the problem-solving discussions which are so central to her teaching.

The present chapter shows that the gaps in understanding Johanna and I both faced were much larger. In order to take on the 'school science' of the guidelines, Johanna would have needed to learn new subject content, and would have had to believe more in the value of science. As it was, she was rather too sceptical to make the effort to bridge the gap between her horizons of understanding and the notion of teaching implicit in the guidelines. Instead, we both bridged the gaps in our understanding by changing school science into something more familiar to us. For me, this meant using some of the patterns of teaching I carried forward from my English teaching, and for Johanna it meant using science as an opportunity to pursue her larger goal of helping students become independent learners.

The series of gaps in understanding we faced, described in the stories in Chapters 3 and 4, were overcome through a process of trial and error, and through many hours of discussion about alternative courses of action. In the final two chapters, I turn my attention to a more analytical discussion of the process by which these new understandings were formed, and the constraints within which the understandings were constructed.

NOTES

1. Here I refer to *Science 7* and *Science 8*, two detailed and practical
    sets of lesson plans designed to meet the requirements of the Pro-
    vincial Intermediate Science Guideline, jointly published by a con-
    sortium of Toronto school boards.

Chapter 5

Reflection

The preceding three chapters have described some of the carefully polished and practised lessons from Johanna's repertoire and followed our experience of teaching writing and science together. As we taught these lessons, our understanding of teaching was in a gradual process of change. Thus far, the account of these changes has been in the context of stories about these lessons, and the argument which has been developed has concentrated on capturing a sense of the temporal, experiential and biographical basis for Johanna's patterns of teaching, choice of content and resolutions to dilemmas of education and control. In this chapter, the approach will be more analytic. Considering all of the changes described in the case study, how may they be characterized? What sorts of dimensions and categories are useful in describing the range of ways in which these changes in understanding of teaching were accomplished?

The word most frequently connected with changes in professional knowledge is 'reflection'. In ordinary language, the word reflection suggests serious and sober thought at some distance from action and has connotations similar to 'meditation' and 'introspection'. It is a mental process which takes place out of the stream of action, looking forward or (usually) back to actions that have taken place. One says, for example: 'On reflection, I realized that . . .'. The word reflection also carries a submerged metaphor, an implied comparison between human understanding and reflections in a mirror. Just as we know that a mirror allows us to see our physical selves as other see us, we hope that the mirror of reflection will allow us to understand ourselves or our circumstances in new ways. The educational uses of the term have carried forward and built on this ordinary language sense of reflection in a wide variety of ways, perhaps so wide as to make the term unusable without careful redefinition. The noun 'reflection' and its adjectival form 'reflective' seems to have been applied to whatever it is that people most admire: reflective action (Dewey, 1933; Berlack and Berlack, 1981), reflective teaching (Zeichner and Liston, 1987; Cruickshank *et al.*, 1981), reflective learning (Boyd and Fales, 1983), reflective practitioners (Schon, 1983, 1987), and reflective practice (Sergiovanni, 1985).

This chapter attempts to clear a conceptual path through the variety of ways in which the term *reflection* has been employed. Like the rest of this study, the argument will be driven by the fine-grained texture of the case study data. The principle I have followed in developing the categories which appear below is to be as *inclusive* as possible. The categories attempt to represent the full range of reflection which appears in the field records of this study. To this end, I offer two dimensions of reflection, the *interests* and *forms* of reflection. These two dimensions are developed from the work of Habermas (1971) and Schon (1983, 1987) respectively.[1] The term *interests* refers to the goal or end in view of an act of reflection: is the goal of reflection fidelity to some theory or practice; or deeper and clearer personal understanding; or professional problem-solving; or critique of the conditions of professional action? *Forms* refers to the characteristics of the act: is it a matter of introspection, of thinking and feeling; of replaying or rehearsing professional action; of systematic enquiry into action; or of spontaneous action? These dimensions, it will be argued, are both different and complementary. A particular act of reflection thus has both an interest and a form, and in principle all reflective acts may be described in terms of both dimensions. The way in which these dimensions are related may be suggested by the four-by-four matrix of Figure 5.1.

As the 16 boxes in this figure suggest, it is – at least in principle – possible to describe the intersection of each of the four forms and interests. For example, one might use a form of reflection such as enquiry into action with the end in view of critique, or problem-solving, or personal growth, or technical fidelity to theory. Equally, one might serve a critical interest by introspection, or by rehearsing a range of options, or by a process of enquiry, or through some spontaneous discovery made in the midst of professional action. In the discussion of Johanna's reflection which follows, I first describe the four interests and then connect these with the four forms of reflection.

FORMS

	Introspection	Replay and rehearsal	Enquiry	Spontaneity
Technical				
Personal				
Problematic				
Critical				

INTERESTS

Figure 5.1 Forms and interests of reflection

REFLECTION AND INTERESTS

It has become customary in the educational literature to make distinctions about interests according to three traditions of enquiry, often using a form of words drawn from Jurgen Habermas's theory of 'knowledge-constitutive interests'. Habermas (1971) distinguishes between the interests of the empirical-analytic sciences, the hermeneutic-historical sciences and the critical sciences. Thus, a series of studies which have attempted to review and reconceptualize fields within education have made similar three-way distinctions.[2] Habermas associates each of the forms of enquiry with a cognitive interest: empirical-analytic enquiry with technical control by discovering rule-like regularities in an objective world; historical-hermeneutic sciences with practical control through understanding and communication; and critical sciences with emancipation through critical reflection on the conditions of social life. This chapter builds on Habermas's framework, following the *technical* and *critical* interests he distinguished and separating the practical interest into two categories, a *personal* interest and a *problematic* interest. Both of these latter interests share Habermas's sense that the historical-hermeneutic sciences serve the interest of practical control, but what I have called the personal interest emphasizes the personal meaning of situations and the problematic interest emphasizes problem-solving in professional work.[3] The range of *interests* of reflection are represented graphically in Figure 5.2.

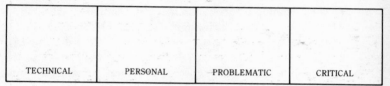

Figure 5.2 Interests of reflection

Technical Interest

The technical interest, an interest in controlling the world by attending to rule-like regularities, is a powerful force in education. It stands behind quantitative research into effective schools and teachers, competency-based teacher evaluation, and much of the research into curriculum implementation. Key issues in technical reflection include fidelity of teachers' practice to some set of empirically or theoretically derived standards and the development of technical skills of teaching. The kind of reflection required in a programme of teacher development based on Madeline Hunter's model of teaching (1983), for example, emphasizes fidelity to the propositional knowledge of the model and attention to the conditions under which each principle ought to be applied.[4] Similarly, there is a technical interest in Cruickshank *et al.*'s (1981) 'reflective teaching', a programme of initial teacher education using a kind of peer or micro teaching. The lesson content, objectives, time allocation and materials are all predetermined, and what is 'reflective' is the discussion among peers and with instructors which follows each peer teaching episode.[5]

In all of the discussions I had with Johanna during a year of collaborative work, there were no clear examples of reflection with such technical interests. In general, Johanna was suspicious of the plans and programmes promoted by her school board and unimpressed by the possibility that she would improve her teaching by following prescriptions of people who were no longer involved in classroom teaching. The closest Johanna came to using propositional knowledge during the life of the study was to refer, several times, to her reading of a pair of books by Thomas Gordon, *Teacher Effectiveness Training* (1974) and *Parent Effectiveness Training* (1970). On the day we first talked about the possibility of participation in a collaborative study, she mentioned that she had recently read one of these books and that it had made a substantial impact on her (8 March, p. 38). Much later, when she was planning a curriculum night she considered looking in these books for activities which might help parents understand her approach to problem-solving with their children (1 November, p. 368). She had come to these books at a time when she was trying to improve her communication with her daughter, and thought of them as symbolic of the changes she had been making as a teacher in the time just before we met:

> *Johanna*   I found the books the summer before you came and they had really changed the way I was working with kids. I found that I was having tremendous difficulty here – tremendous success in many areas but also tremendous difficulty.... I really wanted to be here and I was trying to figure out how I was going to do that.

> (21 November, p. 464)

Johanna had not attended a training programme using this approach, and she did not make detailed references to skills or principles she had drawn from these books, but they had come to symbolize something special and important about her philosophy of education and the approach to children she had been trying to bring to Community School. She rarely talked about teaching in terms of skills, preferring to talk of 'tricks' which she might trade with other teachers at, for example, drama conferences:

> For instance, working in groups of three I have got in my bag of tricks different things I can have them do with the same information. I can have the kids sitting back to back so that they can't see each other while they are talking, and both doing a running monologue about how they are feeling at the same time. It's another way of

approaching the same problem. I can switch and have
them do whole group work, and if kids are finding it too
hard, too embarrassing, I can take the focus of that and
put it somewhere else. . . . You have to have those skills
and that's why I go to drama workshops, because people
will teach me different things to do with kids, things
that I wouldn't have tried that work brilliantly. And
once that becomes part of your repertoire, then you can
trot that out at any time.

(9 August, pp. 112–13)

The kind of reflection involved in trading these tricks, of course,
barely fits the notion of technical reflection. Her interest was not in
fidelity to prior theory or practice, but in expanding her repertoire.
And as Johanna pointed out in this same discussion, 'You only take
it in as it relates to your own life, anyway.'

Personal Interest

Much more common in Johanna's work was reflection with a personal
interest, an interest in connecting experience with her understanding
of her own life. Such a personal interest in reflection informs Connelly and Clandinin's narrative method in teacher education (1986a,
1986b, 1987, 1988). Narrative, they explain, is 'the study of how
humans make meaning of experience by endlessly telling and retelling
stories about themselves that both refigure the past and the create
purposes in the future' (1988, p. 24). Johanna told many stories about
herself which explained the biographical connections between her
experience and her actions, and which shaped her sense of how she
ought to act in the future. She talked, for example, about the biographical roots of her very earnest and serious approach to teaching. As a child at primary school she felt that her job was to be
intelligent, helpful and well behaved, and she took life very seriously:

That all came from the fact that I was the child after a
Down's Syndrome kid, and I think that when I went into
that school I was a kid with a purpose. I knew exactly
what I had to do in life. These were things that were
expected of me and I knew really clearly what I had to

153

do. I was really serious. I can remember my Dad . . .
saying to me, 'Who's the funny one in the group?' And I
said, 'Well, I guess it's me.' And he just laughed. He said,
'You!' as if it was totally impossible that I would be
funny. And I thought, 'Oh, I guess I'm not funny.' But
there must have been some of the big me – that loves a
joke – in the little me. I still do take life very seriously,
and I don't think that there's anything I can do to change
that. That's who I am.

(2 November, pp. 139-40)

In the past, one of the consequences of her serious approach to
teaching has been that Johanna has sometimes taken on more
commitments – shows, parental interviews, problem-solving with
students – than she could manage, and that she has often felt
guilty and dissatisfied that she has not lived up to her hopes and
dreams. In her private life she had been trying to give up the
debilitating expectation that life ought always be perfect, and to
take more pleasure in the present. Her strategy has been to surround
herself with friends who supported her to appreciate the moment – the
journey – rather than the destination (29 June, pp. 59-60). As she
looked back at the experience of reading the field notes and early
drafts of this study, she realized that she had been making some progress on this personal and professional issue (5 November, p. 401; 17
February, pp. 438-8). She was now more ready to accept that she was
a good teacher and less inclined to be critical of herself. Our collaboration, she said, came at 'exactly the right time' for her, and it had cap-
tured the 'artistry' of her work:

I was embarking on something totally new, I was having
to rethink everything, I was feeling very open to
understanding and being willing to accept my being a
good teacher and not being so hard on myself as a
teacher. It fit perfectly. Although I have always been
interested in looking at what I do, this was probably the
best time to catch me. . . . It is as if someone had been
able to capture the artistry of what I was doing and that
felt good to know that it was recorded somewhere. This

thing that I had worked on and honed had actually made it down on paper.

(17 February, pp. 485–6)

Similarly, she talked about the connection between her commitment to helping students to become more independent and her own experience of uncertainty at college during the 'druggy times' of the 1960s:

> It really affects what I do with kids. My feeling about why that time was so absolutely terrifying for so many kids is that the world didn't make any sense to them in terms of their own independence. They were not strong, they were not solid and I certainly wasn't. I'd never been given practice in decision making. I was looking for some sort of meaning for life, for some sort of truth that I was told was very important, and then handed Catholicism. So, for me that was a terrifying time because, although it was very exciting, you were being blown about by winds that were bigger than you and you could be so badly hurt. People were dying, people were going crazy. It was heady, because you finally had your freedom and you were beginning to do things together as a group, but we were such children.

(6 September, p. 144)

Her education and upbringing had not helped Johanna learn to make decisions about her own life, she thought, and this had consequences for her actions as a teacher:

> You don't have to be a baby at 18 and 19 and 20. But our society made us children and kept us children. It is something I feel is terribly dangerous to children. You have to give them the strength to go out and be able to protect themselves and be independent and make it in the world and not be led by peer pressures into stuff that is going to be destructive. So, that experience of being so totally unprepared led to how I feel I ought to deal with kids now.

(6 September, p. 145)

For Johanna, one of the effects of personal reflection is that it supports her sense of agency, her sense that she controls her own destiny. From her father – 'who always wanted a boy', she said – she received permission to be the one who decides what she should do, to be the wage earner, to take control rather than be controlled by others (2 September, p. 143). Subsequently, and through a series of changes in country of residence and subject speciality as a teacher, she has struggled to construct a safe and comfortable working environment. At Community School, she felt that she had achieved the freedom to do what she wanted to do as a teacher:

> Right now I have the freedom to really do what I want to
> do with the kids, which is an unbelievable freedom. Very,
> very few teachers have that freedom to work in an
> environment of people that I know and love, and do what
> I want to do without having too much interference from
> people who are trying to tell me what I ought to be
> doing. I am in a wonderful situation at the moment. If I
> can make it less work for myself and less exhausting,
> then it is a great position to be in.

(9 August, p. 116)

Problematic Interest

Unlike reflection with a personal interest, which connects biography and experience, the problematic interest is concerned with resolution of the problems of professional action. This is the interest most fully represented in Schon's work on reflection (1983, 1987). The problems of most concern to Schon are problems which fall outside the established technical knowledge of a profession: cases, for example, which are not 'in the book' (1987, p. 34) and situations which are 'uncertain, unique or conflicted' (1987, p. 35). Such problem-solving may take place in informal experiments which take place while it is still possible to alter the outcomes of action – Schon's reflection-in-action – or after the event, as in Schon's reflection-on-action. In either case, his interest is primarily in the situations that learners or practitioners already see as problematic: occasions where people are surprised by what happens and are moved to rethink their professional practice.

There were many examples of reflection with a problematic interest as Johanna and I taught writing and science together. Some of this reflection was what Schon calls reflection-on-action. We talked, for example, about problems with content, alternative patterns of teaching, ways of pursuing independent learning goals, and the problems we had with particular groups and students. More interesting, and less well documented in the educational literature, are those examples of the reflection with a problematic interest which Schon calls reflection-in-action.[6] The following story, from a writing lesson on 28 October 1988, provides several such examples. This lesson was part of a long sequence of lessons during which Johanna's classes prepared the text for their own illustrated books.

That worked well About two weeks into the illustrated book project, Johanna had asked students to complete the text of their books and to be ready to hand them in. When she announced to the students in Group 1 that she was coming round the class to check, some of the students attempted to talk her out of collecting the work, claiming that they didn't know about the deadline or shifting the blame to some third party. Johanna was irritated because she had planned to take the scripts home and correct them before students started to do their illustrations. How could she do this if students were not all finished? She took out her mark book to record those who were ready and who were not.

> *Johanna* How many people are done? I am going to take this down. A little language mark. [*Writing in a column of her mark book.*] 'Story by due date'. If you have done what was required for today – no excuses count – if you were done by today, raise your hand.

> (28 October, p. 358)

Just as she realized that only five of the sixteen students present had done as she asked, a student arrived with a message from the school secretary, asking her to check the form which she had prepared for students' interim reports from the school. Johanna seized the opportunity offered by this interruption, connected the mark she had just allocated for meeting the due date to the interim report, and began reading aloud from the interim report form:

Listen up. Interim reports are coming out soon. Here's what the interim report which is going home on Monday is going to say. You could be in the 'A' category: *This student is making good use of Community School*, or you could be in the 'B' category: *This student is progressing satisfactorily. The check marks indicate areas which the teachers consider require special attention: homework, behaviour, punctuality.* Punctuality! 'C': *A teacher who places a check mark in one of these boxes does so because he or she feels grave concern for this aspect of the student's learning and would like to discuss the matter: Math skills, reading skills, need for supervision, ability to meet deadlines.* Ability to meet deadlines! Five of you passed test number 1, ability to meet deadlines!

(28 October, p. 359)

While students were finding their calendars and marking in their weekend homework, I walked across to Johanna, who had been sitting on a stool on the rug in the centre of the room. She turned to me:

Johanna	What shall we do?
Bill	I was just going to suggest that one way of saving you some marking time at home would be for the two of us . . .
Johanna	To travel round?
Bill	. . . to read their stuff while the students who are ready continue with their reading.
Johanna	OK, I'll let the five students who are done do their illustrations. [*To class*:] OK, we are going to have two different lessons happen today. The first lesson is for the five people who are ready – and this is what you would all be doing if you were ready – can start to work in their sketchbooks on the illustrations for each page.

(28 October, p. 359)

While Johanna moved around the room helping students with proof-reading, I sat at one table and worked through several students' stories in detail. At the end of the lesson, Johanna said, 'That worked well. We can keep helping them while they do their illustrations. This would be better than taking it home to check.' I replied, 'Exactly, the point is that it gives us the chance to teach at the point of error rather than taking it home and practising our own spelling and punctuation.

* * *

There are two instances of the form of problematic reflection Schon calls reflection-in-action and one of reflection-on-action in this story. First, when Johanna was interrupted by the student carrying sample report forms just as she realized that only five of her 16 students had met the absolute deadline she had set, she seized the moment and connected the two events. Like Schon's example of a jazz player's reflection-in-action, she smoothly integrated a new element into her ongoing performance (Schon, 1987, p. 30). Second, when she realized the impact this would have on her lesson plan, we had a quick conversation about what to do next. As in Schon's example of reflection-in-action as he built his garden gate (Schon, 1987, p. 27), we were surprised by what happened and invented a new procedure in the midst of action. Had Johanna been on her own, she might have taken a moment to have a similar, silent conversation with herself. Third, as the lesson closed we swapped stories about our responses to this unexpected turn of events. As we reflected *on* what had happened, Johanna commented that the split-second decision we made (our reflection-*in*-action) had worked well, and I observed that this pattern of teaching might help solve a problem she had been worrying about – finding a way to help students with their sentence construction. Not only had a moment of reflection led to resolution of a particular problem of the day, it had opened up possibilities for a more general improvement in her pattern for teaching writing. In the moment of action, Johanna and I had different reasons for coming to the same resolution to this problem: for her, splitting the class represented an appropriate consequence for students who had or had not met her deadlines; for me it made time for teaching at the point of error. By the end of this lesson, when she said 'That worked well', she had realized that allowing students to spread across different stages of a longer task gave her time to teach individually and at the point of error.

159

Critical Interest

Although perhaps the least familiar interest for reflection among teachers, if the reports of Jackson (1968) and Lortie (1975) are to be believed, what I am calling critical reflection is the most comprehensively theorized of the four interests of reflection.[7] The essence of the critical interest in reflection is that it involves questioning taken-for-granted thoughts, feelings and actions. Through such reflection, teachers may confront and perhaps transcend the constraints they otherwise perceive as normal or natural. Critical reflection begins with the assumption that reality is socially constructed and that people can act to influence the conditions in which they find themselves. To this end, critical reflection involves considering who benefits from current practices, how these practices might be changed, and personal or political action to secure changes in the conditions of classroom work.

Active learning It was not always easy for Johanna and I to find time for reflection at Community School. Often we would have lunch together at the bistro across the road from the school and there, freed from the press of students passing through the staffroom asking questions and looking for company, we were able to talk about a wider range of issues. We talked at length, for example, about the idea of a good school and about the possibilities of educational change (21 September; 25 October; 8 November). In one of these discussions, Johanna talked about a school board seminar she and Miles had just attended. The topic was 'active learning', a major local priority in the year of the study. She was enthusiastic about the workshop, partly because she agreed with what the speaker had been saying and partly because he had said it in front of her principal:

> *Johanna* Miles' comment was that what he said we all
> knew fifteen years ago – but he said it to a
> gathering of every single teacher in this area.
> He said it in front of the superintendent and
> our principal. He'd been hired to come and say
> it, so obviously it was approved of. What they
> said was exactly what you and I have been
> saying, which is that you cannot pour
> knowledge into a kid. What a kid actually

learns will depend on how actively involved in
his own education and problem-solving he is
and that to delineate the number of minutes
[per week] that you have him doing a certain
thing doesn't give you any information about
what has happened educationally for that child.

So it was a vindication and I looked around
to see if [the principal] was listening to that
little bit because it is what we have been saying
to him.

(25 October, pp. 342–3)

I was glad that she felt vindicated by what the speaker had said
in front of her principal, but I wondered aloud what other people might
have made of the session. There was obviously a good fit between
Johanna's teaching and the idea that was being promoted. I wondered,
however, whether such a session would have been any use to a teacher
with a more skills-oriented approach to teaching. Did talking about
'active learning' at a workshop make any difference to such teachers?
My question seemed a little pessimistic to Johanna, who knew how
much she had changed as a teacher in recent years. She had, she said,
spent many years 'trying to impose the way I felt things ought to be
on kids, instead of listening to where they were'. Perhaps such sessions could help other people to move along the path towards active
learning. My reaction was that such sessions would have no impact
on Johanna's own teaching:

Bill   What they are ignoring is how deeply connected
what you did today is to your history. You are
an 'activity' teacher. When you get a subject
which lends itself in other people's hands to
giving lectures and notes, you turn it into an
activity subject. Invariably, you go for the
kid's personal difficulty not the subject content.

(25 October, p. 343)

We realized that we had a fundamental difference of opinion about the value and the possibility of making a particular teaching method compulsory, and were interested to explore our differences.

> *Bill*   It's to do with the difference between being powerfully convinced that for you it is the best thing to do, and insisting that other people do the same.

> *Johanna*   You feel that because it happens to be right for me, that I should not therefore jump to the conclusion that it would be right for everybody?

> (25 October, p. 344)

This was what I had meant, and I went on to suggest that there was more at stake here than personal preferences. What happened to a person with a skills-oriented view of teaching, such as a colleague of Johanna whose history left him poorly equipped to take on 'active learning'?

> *Bill*   So, when someone stands up in the staffroom at the beginning of the year and announces that the Board has three priorities this year and one is active learning, what goes on inside [Johanna's colleague] is that he wipes off the Board or he feels guilty. Neither of those is healthy for the system or the teacher. My sense is that alongside the announcement that the Board is interested in active learning there needs to be space for something that a skills-oriented person can do well.

> (25 October, p. 345)

The difference between us was not in our vision of good schooling but in our sense of the practical and ethical problems of communicating our vision to other people. Johanna, perhaps more committed to the value of active learning than concerned about what it would be like to have someone trying to impose a different teaching method on her, responded with an assertion of the need for change and a practical example of the way she would approach it:

> *Johanna*   I still feel that there is a way. When you are at teachers' college you do courses which are theoretically supposed to help you understand the human mind. I would like to teach those courses by having the people actually being involved in the technique of active listening. . . . To give you an example, yesterday I was in this drama group with a guy from England. I watched what happened in the group. One of the people in my group was very bossy and I was put off by her approach. I could sense that there were several people in the group who had never done any drama before and were very nervous. Because of what I know about how to listen to people, I was able to get the group working happily together. . . . Now I could teach that to teachers and that would be a very worthwhile thing, because that's what we do – work in groups – so I would say that would be a way of changing people.

> (25 October, p. 347)

* * *

In conversations such as this, one interest in reflection may be dominant without other interests being abandoned. Here the interest is primarily critical, because it concerns the application of power over teachers and the possibility that well-meaning educational change activities may close down some people's opportunities to teach in ways that are consistent with their own biography and experience. But alongside this interest in the ethical conditions of the use of power is Johanna's personal interest in ways of teaching that are biographically appropriate for her, and my personal interest in the need for plurality in educational change. More than this, the critical interest in the discussion is pursued through the example of a practical problem and the technical skills Johanna used in overcoming it.

The notion of critical reflection developed in this section draws directly on the emancipatory interest that Habermas has introduced to the debate about reflection, in that it is concerned with critique of the social structures within which people act. Because the examples are drawn from the case study data rather than representing ideal types, however, they lack the political edge which proponents of critical reflection may have in mind.[8]

FORMS OF REFLECTION

These four *interests* of reflection account for the range of reasons teachers might have for reflection, but they do not help elaborate the range of ways in which changes in understanding and action take place. To explore the latter issue more closely, I now turn to the dimension of *forms* of reflection. This set of categories represents a range from reflection as a process of thinking or feeling separated from action to reflection as a process which takes place in the moment of action. Between these extremes stand two categories of reflection which deal with both thought and action. (See Figure 5.3.)

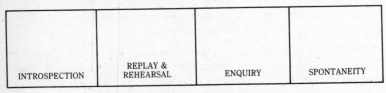

| INTROSPECTION | REPLAY & REHEARSAL | ENQUIRY | SPONTANEITY |

Figure 5.3 Forms of reflection

The reason for arraying forms of reflection across this dimension is that the forms ought to allow for the range between tacit and explicit knowledge. Some of Johanna's knowledge as a teacher is tacit and embodied in her practice, in patterns such as the way she conducts class discussions or conferences, the way she begins and ends lessons, and the way she teaches guitar to whole-class groups. Other parts of Johanna's knowledge are more explicit, such as her content knowledge in music and art, and the hopes and dreams for teaching which impel her to work with students' feelings and to prefer content which is relevant to their interests. Some of her knowledge is not knowledge at all – in the sense of knowledge as justified true belief – but a series of unanswered questions on which she is still working, such as how she can best help students to become more independent and how she can find a comfortable way of teaching science.

Consequently, this dimension ranges between forms of reflection appropriate to the two extremes of tacit and explicit knowledge. At one extreme, reflection may be a conscious process conducted at some distance from the stream of action. This form of reflection, which involves both thinking and feeling, may be called reflection as *introspection*. At the other extreme stands a form of reflection so bound up in the moment of action that there is no conscious awareness of thinking about the action, a form of reflection which may be called reflection as *spontaneity*. The two intermediate categories are reflection as *replay and rehearsal*, the sort of reflection which might involve a teacher thinking or talking about events that have happened or might happen in the future, and reflection as *enquiry*, a form of reflection which involves thinking and acting in a deliberate process of enquiry. Whereas Schon's dichotomy of reflection-in-action and reflection-on-action accounts for this range in two forms of reflection, the remainder of this chapter explores these four forms of reflection and connects the forms of reflection with the four interests already established.

Introspection

Introspection, which involves looking inwards and reconsidering one's thoughts and feelings about some issue, is the closest form of reflection to the ordinary language sense of reflection as contemplation or meditation. Boyd and Fales (1983), for example, talk about 'reflective learning', a process of 'internally examining and exploring an issue of concerns triggered by an experience, which creates and clarifies meaning in terms of self, and which results in a changed conceptual perspective' (1983, p. 100). For Boyd and Fales, introspection clearly has a personal interest, but this need not be the case. Mezirow (1981), for example, has outlined a process of introspection with a critical interest which he calls 'perspective transformation'. By confronting the psychological and cultural assumptions which constrain the way people see things, he argues, they may transform their perceptions of the world. He describes a series of levels of reflectivity which include affective reflectivity, which refers to the process of becoming aware of how we feel about our preconceptions and habits of action, and psychic reflectivity which leads a person, for example, to consider unresolved childhood dilemmas.

In Johanna's case, most of the introspection she shared with me had a personal interest: the relationship between her family of origin and her attitudes to life and work; the relationship between her experience of the 'druggy times' of the 1960s and her determination to help students learn to accept more responsibility for their own decision-making; the effect of learning the clarinet as an adult on her attitudes to praise in music teaching. Less often, this introspection led to reflection with a critical intent, such as in the following story about her experience of growing up during the second wave of feminism:

> There was an interesting episode in high school with my two crazy friends, who certainly were not the twin-set-and-pearls style. One of them was on the committee where they could elect the Prom Queen, and my name came up. My friend told me about it later. She said, 'I couldn't do it to you Johanna, I just couldn't. I got you out of it.' At the time I had the feeling that it was bizarre that I would want recognition from that world, of being the female symbol of sexuality. I was saved by my friend but I wasn't sure I was saved. I wanted it, yet it would have grated. The same sort of thing continued at college. I didn't know where I belonged. At the fraternity, one of the things they did was hold a huge parade and they would find girls to march along the parade wearing short skirts and looking sexy. I can remember doing that and thinking, 'Nah. This is not where I want to be. This is me on a platter, served up.'
>
> ... It was very hard for me to find a way of being feminine and sexy without going into that world where women are objects. So for a long time I couldn't pass through a cosmetic department in a big department store without feeling that the women who stood behind the counters would recognize that I was not one of them. I wasn't a type who could do that. Somehow I would like to have been able to be female in that way, whatever that was. I had to find that much later, how to be feminine and not be a possession.

(2 September, p. 143)

The interest in this introspection is critical, in the sense that it relates to the struggle she has had to find a way of being feminine without being a sex object, but the story would be too private for some people to tell. At an early stage in this study, fearful that I would exceed the boundaries beyond which a researcher ought not pry, I was inclined to close down some of the more delicate and personal aspects of introspection. During a life-history interview, for example, I stopped myself in the middle of a line of questioning to ask whether I had exceeded those reasonable boundaries:

Bill   Part of me – the therapist part – feels like saying, 'Can you tell me some more about that', and asking you to give an example and go into your inner life. It just occurred to me as you said that that it is not my role. It's not what I am doing here. I am just trying to get a good, clean, clear story that gives a sense of who you are, so that people can understand what you do in the classroom. . . . It's not my task to help you understand the way you are. I would need a license to do that.

(2 September, p. 140)

Not only did Johanna reject the possibility that I could get a good, clean, clear story ('Stories don't come good and clean and clear', she said), but she also rejected my artificial separation of the roles of therapist, teacher and researcher:

Johanna   Well, *there's* an issue, because I don't think so. That's a real teaching issue. That means that I don't have a license to do what I do with the kids, to help them understand why they are . . . and you are my friend, and I'm your friend. I would help you, we all do that for each other. Which really means that therapists are an artificial construction of society because we don't do it enough for each other.

(2 September, p. 141)

In our work together we reached this explicit agreement to include introspection which might be thought by some to be too private and personal, but that might not always be the case in other research projects. This agreement was reached in the context of a teacher–researcher relationship which had been developed with particular care, and involved a teacher who was more than usually open and forthcoming. Judging by the reluctance of other teachers on the staff to make any comments on the early field notes I shared with them (8 March, p. 38; 11 March, p. 46; 29 June, p. 60), other teachers might not have been as forthcoming. Some teachers might regard the depth of introspection required in, for example, journal writing or a research project such as this study, as beyond the reasonable boundaries of research or professional development.[9]

Replay and Rehearsal

Replay and rehearsal is a form of reflection which involves teachers' discourse about events that have occurred or the possibility of future actions. As teachers talk to their colleagues (or write) about their work they make sense of surprising classroom events, draw provisional generalizations which may inform their future practice, make plans for action, and affirm their values. This form of reflection is one step closer to action than introspection, but still stands at some distance from the deliberate movement between action and reflection which characterizes enquiry. The conditions of teachers' classroom work – immediacy, multidimensionality, simultaneity, unpredictability[10] – mean that it is rarely possible for teachers to think or talk about the meaning of their experience or their immediate plans while they are still in what Schon calls 'the action present' (1983, p. 62). More often, teachers are fully immersed in what they are doing, too busy juggling burning swords to reflect consciously on what they are doing while there is still time to make a difference to the situation at hand.

Unlike the 'virtual worlds' which Schon describes in the profession of architecture (1987, pp. 75–8), it is not easy to construct realistic models of teaching where teachers may practise and refine their actions.[11] Real classrooms are usually too busy to allow teachers to step outside the stream of action and so, most often, the meaning-making takes place outside the classroom: in the hallway, in the staff-room, on the journey home, over dinner or at teachers' conferences. On these occasions teachers tell stories about their experiences, replaying events in a form which outsiders may dismiss as unreflective 'war stories'. Replaying the events of a school day and rehearsing alternative courses of action, however, is essential to making meaning of the experience.

In Johanna's case, there are many examples of such reflection. Indeed, one of the advantages for Johanna of our collaborative work was that she had someone to tell these stories to. Garth, her spouse, was very patient in listening to her stories but he didn't appreciate them in the way I did:

> *Johanna*   I have never had anyone who was really as
> interested in what I was doing as I was, and
> here was somebody who was *totally* interested!
> How many people does that happen to in life! I
> mean, can you imagine if someone came up to
> you and said, 'I really want to know all about
> you. Tell me in complete detail.' . . . No matter
> how much Garth tries, he could never be as
> interested in the actual machinations as you
> were. That was wonderful. It worked so well.
>
> (17 February, p. 486)

Such replays and rehearsals of experience may proceed with a technical, personal, problematic or critical interest. When Shulman (1987, p. 19) talks about reflection, for example, he describes it as when a teacher 'looks back at the teaching and learning that has occurred, and reconstructs, reenacts, and/or recaptures the events, the emotions, and the accomplishments' of teaching. It is through this process, Shulman points out, that professionals learn from experience. In Shulman's sense of reflection, the interest is essentially technical:[12]

> it is likely that reflection is not merely a disposition (as in,
> 'she's such a reflective person!') or a set of strategies, but
> also the use of particular kinds of analytical knowledge
> brought to bear on one's work. . . . Central to this process
> will be a review of the teaching in comparison to the ends
> that were sought.
>
> (Shulman, 1987, p. 19)

169

Other teacher educators and researchers, more concerned with a personal interest than with fidelity of means to ends, have encouraged teachers to tell stories about their work and lives in order that they may reshape their understanding of their past, present and future (see Connelly and Clandinin, 1988; Butt and Raymond, 1987). Similarly, researchers with a critical interest, such as Tripp (1987) and Berlack and Berlack (1981) have argued that teachers should talk or write about their experience in order to understand it in new ways.

In our collaborative work, however, the larger part of the replay and rehearsal of classroom events was reflection with a problematic interest. Johanna and I often talked in very concrete terms about the meaning of events we had just experienced, or about the possibilities for future action. These conversations often involved verbatim rehearsals of what we would say to a class. The story below describes a typical case of replay after the event.

That's it for tricks Picture us sitting in the quietest place we could find, the fire escape steps, interrupted from time to time by a class from the junior division of the school moving up or down from the playground (8 November, pp. 414–19). I had lately been reading Gramsci (1971), and was wondering whether his notion of common sense, that unreflective knowledge which is composed of both good sense and bad sense, might be a useful analytic construct for this study. Johanna had read a commentary on Gramsci and a working paper I had prepared on common sense, and thought it was all a little disconnected from reality (7 November, p. 412). I had been talking about some of the common-sense qualities of the teachers' knowledge I had noticed at the school and mentioned that I had been surprised how context-specific my own knowledge of teaching was:

Bill	It's like knowledge of what will work disappears if you change classes, or subjects, or – in my case – countries. Or if you have a bit of a break.
Johanna	Like summer? Which explains why I was terrified on the first day of school, although I have been doing this for twenty years. The break totally destroys your sense that you can do it again. The thing about teaching that every teacher knows is that it is like handling animals:

the kids, if they know that you are scared, will
be in control. So it's a confidence trick. It will
work only if you can convince them that you can
make it work. This is something that every
teacher in their heart of hearts knows. Really,
this is dicey at times. There is no way you could
control a group of kids who didn't want to be
controlled. It has to do with a tremendous
number of tricks you pull out of your bag,
things that you know about child psychology,
and every teacher has their own bag of tricks.
There is always a chance that those tricks may
not work. You have to keep going through the
bag.

(8 November, p. 418)

My response to this image of teachers' knowledge as a bag of tricks was
to think of several concrete cases where we had needed to dig deep into
the bag.

Bill	With some kids, like Mark, you just get to the point where you think: 'My bag is empty. That's it for tricks.'
Johanna	Yes.
Bill	Then you get a case like Luke, just then. When you approach him, you don't know what's going to happen. You think that you can talk him into [rewriting his illustrated book], but you don't know whether he is going to pull a face and wipe you off for a month.
Johanna	Yes, because I had to watch his face really closely and judge what to say next. I was looking for the recognition in his eyes that he knew it was rubbish. That didn't come as quickly as I thought it would come with Luke. He obviously had more investment in the story than I thought.

171

> Bill   I thought it would come as soon as I said, 'You
>   are a smart guy, you can do better than this.'
>
> Johanna We managed to pull ourselves out of that,
>   having taken the wrong tack to start with, to
>   think of other tricks we knew.
>
>   (8 November, pp. 418–19)

* * *

In such ways, Johanna and I spent dozens of hours of spares, lunch times and breaks exploring our understanding of events we had been too busy enacting to reflect on at the time. Because our teaching was such a stream of unreflected experience, we needed to replay these stories in order to make meaning of the experiences we shared. These stories may not be very technical, they were probably boring to the friends and spouses who had no experience of teaching, but they were stories which needed to be told if the experience were to contribute to our development as teachers.

Enquiry

Unlike replay and rehearsal and introspection, where reflection takes place at some distance from action, enquiry is a form of reflection which involves both action and discourse about action. More than this, it involves a process of deliberate movement between action and discourse. In the educational literature on reflection, the kind of deliberate process here called enquiry has been described and theorized by Carr and Kemmis (1986) in their work on action research. They describe action research as a 'self-reflective spiral of cycles of planning, acting, observing and reflecting' (1986, p. 162). In addition to describing the form in which action research takes place, they link it with the critical interest for reflection. Like the introspection involved in Mezirow's perspective transformation, and the replay and rehearsal involved in Berlack and Berlack's critical enquiry, Carr and Kemmis's stipulative definition of action research presumes that the end in view of reflection is emancipatory educational and social change.

The form of reflection here called enquiry, however, may also be undertaken with technical, personal and problematic interests. Grundy (1987, pp. 149–50), for example, describes a scenario where the action research cycle of planning, observation, action and reflection is followed, but the end in view is fidelity to already established practices of an activity-based mathematics programme. The descriptions of curriculum planning by Connelly and Clandinin (1988, pp. 170–86) also include a deliberate movement between discourse and action, but in the case they describe the enquiry is shaped by a personal interest. Enquiry shaped by a problematic interest is well documented in Schon's work on reflection-in-action and in particular what he calls the 'reflective conversation', a process of conscious on-the-spot experimentation in the action-present which occurs when practitioners try to resolve the unfamiliar problems which confront them in their professional practice (Schon, 1987, pp. 26–31).

In the collaborative work Johanna and I did in teaching writing and science, much of our reflection was shaped by problematic interests. Unlike Johanna's music and art lessons, where she was working from a long-established repertoire, in science and writing we had to talk about each step before we could proceed. In science, especially, where neither of us had taught the subject before, we could not rely on what Schutz and Luckmann (1973) called 'the natural attitude', but had to find a way of connecting the new subject with our established patterns of teaching. Inside this larger cycle of enquiry we used all four of the forms of reflection which are identified in this chapter. The way in which the other three forms may be embedded in a larger cycle of enquiry may be explored through a story drawn from our work together in science. In this case we talked about the content of a lesson Johanna needed to teach and developed a lesson plan; Johanna taught the lesson; we talked about the detail of what she had done and connected this experience to an issue we had been talking about, Johanna's realization that she lacked the content knowledge and commitment required to teach the sort of science recommended in the guideline.

Science is a real mystery to me This story begins one afternoon (7 November) during a swimming lesson. While a specialist teacher took the swimming class, Johanna and I sat in the sun and talked about the next step to take in preparing students for the science assignment we had given them. First we found the section in one of our textbooks that dealt with the assignment tasks we wanted to teach, classification of leaves and the life cycle of animals. As we talked about this material, Johanna wondered why it mattered that students should be able to classify things. We talked for a time about the arbitrariness of the act of classification, that the classification system chosen would then affect the way people saw the world, and the importance of having a system of classification in order to get the world's work done. I suggested that she do an activity like the one in the science guide, asking students to make up a system of classification to explain the objects in the room or a set of objects she chose for them. As we talked about this idea, we both became quite enthusiastic. We began rehearsing aloud the kinds of thing we might say or do – such as having a student among the 'things' to be classified – and laughing together at the little jokes this might lead to. By the end, she said that this sounded like the sort of science lesson I'd like to do. It sounded like this to me, too, and I was sorry not to be there to do it.

I missed the lesson we had planned, but later (8 November) asked Johanna to tell me what had happened.

> *Johanna* I didn't do any more planning for the class or thinking about it than our conversation at the pool. I had a vague idea of where I was going, what I was trying to do and it seemed to me like the kind of lesson I had done enough of that I could just fly with it. I realized that was wrong when I got into Group 1 and had to teach it. The instant that I began to teach it, I realized that it might be beneficial to pretend to be from another planet and to have collected these things we were trying to identify. So I played that game with them, but it was the kind of thing that I really needed to have thought about ahead of time.
>
> (8 November, p. 414)

Although we had talked about what we needed to teach next and planned a way of presenting the ideas, when Johanna began to teach the lesson she realized that she had lost her grip on the lesson we had rehearsed. Instead, she followed an idea she had in class. The first time she used the 'man from Mars' idea it was with one of the relatively easy Grade 7 classes and the game she played led to a reasonably successful lesson. When Johanna tried to repeat her success in the more challenging context of the Grade 8 class she realized that she did not really understand the idea of classification in science which she had set out to teach:

> By the time I did it with the second class, the Grade 8s, I realized that I wasn't really clear what I was trying to teach them about classification. I had a vague idea that what I was trying to do was to let them see that classification is arbitrary, depending on why you are doing the classifying. But that seemed to me to be a really hard concept to imagine the kids getting their heads around. I lacked the conviction that it was going to work. . . . I didn't know enough about classification. I couldn't give them examples of why someone would classify. What divides one species from another? I don't know enough science.

> (8 November, p. 414)

The lesson with the Grade 8s did not go well, but the questions students asked helped her develop some of her own ideas about classification. By the time Johanna taught the third lesson she had developed a clearer sense of the value of classification in science, and in the less-demanding context of a small Grade 7 class the lesson passed quite successfully.

> Anyway, as I went through the three lessons I realized that there were some little things I could teach, such as that scientists actually *did* this, it didn't come from God, and that it had to do with ways of looking at objects and finding similarities and differences. Those things I could teach and I got better at teaching them.

> (8 November, pp. 414–15)

We ended this small cycle of our larger enquiry with a moment of introspection. Moving beyond the replay of details of the lessons, Johanna talked about her lack of content knowledge and commitment in teaching science.

175

>
> *Johanna* It's so completely obvious that I don't know enough science and I haven't taught this way and done this kind of stuff to be a good science teacher.
>
> *Bill* So what's the difference between you and me in this? I obviously haven't taught science. Do I seem to have more depth of knowledge in science?
>
> *Johanna* I think you are more sure of yourself. You are fairly confident that you know as much science as you need to know to be able to help these kids. I don't. Science is a real mystery to me.
>
> (8 November, p. 416)

* * *

This story describes a brief cycle of enquiry, itself part of the larger reflective enquiry into teaching science. In this case Johanna set out to teach a concept she did not really understand. By the time she had finished teaching three classes she had a stronger sense of what there might be worth teaching about the notion of classification in biology. She still, however, lacked the detailed content knowledge of examples from the classification systems biologists use and the purposes these systems serve. Within this cycle of enquiry there are examples of replay and rehearsal – in the lesson planning we did and in the stories Johanna told about her lessons – and of introspection. In addition, the process of learning through experience is also a form of reflection – spontaneity – which is outlined in the next section.

Spontaneity

The fourth and final form of reflection distinguished here is spontaneity, the tacit reflection which takes place within the stream of experience. This is the form of reflection which corresponds with the 'jazz-player' form of Schon's reflection-in-action. In the midst of action, and without turning one's attention back against the stream of experience to become aware of this as action in the world of time and space, teachers seize the moment and change the direction of their action. Cole (1987) has described a similar process, which she calls 'teachers' spontaneous adaptations' to changing circumstances in the classroom. Building on a sense of teachers' action as informed by their professional knowledge but not necessarily consciously known, she defines teachers' spontaneous adaptation as the 'split-second overt manifestations of a covert dialogue ongoing between the teachers' knowledge and their actions' (Cole, 1987, p. 2). As with Schon's jazz player, this is a process of 'reading' and 'flexing' (Hunt, 1976) to students, making small and tacit adjustments to changing circumstances in the classroom.

The tacit quality of spontaneity poses particular problems for a researcher hoping to document the phenomenon. In some cases I noticed changes in direction which Johanna was only aware of after the fact. When we tried to talk about such cases more fully, the task of asking about awareness of a process which is by definition tacit led me to uncomfortable and inconclusive cross-examinations of Johanna. On one occasion, for example, I asked her how she came to make a major digression from the plan she had followed in the first of three similar lessons:

Johanna	In the second class I went into the telephone activity just because I was bored. I thought I'd basically cover the same things, but just do a bit of enrichment in the area of telephone interviewing.
Bill	So, did that occur to you in the break between the lessons?
Johanna	It occurred to me two minutes before I did it.
Bill	It actually occurred to you though? You made a decision, there was a cognitive leap, 'I think I'll go on here and do telephone interviews?' The time passed and you saw a moment and then you started?
Johanna	No, the moment came, I saw it and took it. It occurred to me immediately before I took it.
Bill	You actually did think, 'I will do it' before you did it?
Johanna	I probably did actually. I was thinking about Bob, actually, and a lesson I saw him teach last

> year on telephone interviewing. It occurred to
> me when I got to that section of the IFT
> [independent field trip] discussion that they were
> going to be doing a lot of phoning. I don't know
> when it happened, but I was doing it.

(27 October, pp. 254–5)

As an observer of the two lessons, it was easy for me to notice that there had been a change in plan. In place of a discussion about the rules for setting up an independent field trip there was a role play of the telephone calls students would need to make. But when I asked how the change came about, Johanna was not at all certain what had happened. She might have thought about it, she could certainly remember seeing another teacher use the role-play technique successfully, but she was finally unsure whether or not she had thought about it in advance. Because it was hard for Johanna to reconstruct an account of whether she did or did not move out of the stream of experience to reflect consciously on her options, the remaining examples in this section are drawn from my notes about my own teaching. Having wondered from the beginning of the study how to account for the role of thinking in the moment-by-moment inventions teachers make in the classroom, I was more easily able to report on the phenomenon. In the following story I describe a case where my spontaneous action led to me to an unpredictable and unfamiliar place and I learned more about how to teach science to my Grade 7 classes.

Let's find out During this lesson (6 October), students in Group 2 were introduced to the notion that the formulation of problems is the first step in the scientific method. I used a series of activities from the school board handbook, *Science 7*, and began by asking students to formulate a problem based on their observations about the following:

1. Get down on your knees. Place an elbow against your knee and stretch your arm and fingers out on the floor.
2. Stand a chalk board eraser on the tip of your fingers.
3. Place both of your hands behind your back. Bend over and knock the eraser with your nose without falling over.

4. After doing the activity take a class vote for the
   results. How many males were successful? How many
   females?

I asked the class to read the instructions and write down whether they
thought more boys or girls would be able to knock over the duster.
Overwhelmingly, they seemed to think that it would be the girls.
This was a surprise, and two possible explanations struck me. Either
they had been talking about it in the hall to the other Grade 7 class,
who had just had the same lesson, or they had understood me to
ask whether more boys than girls in this class would be successful.
Something inside me, not quite conscious, told me not to check on the
first possibility. If they heard about it in the hallway, and they knew
that I knew, it would seem silly to continue. Instead, I pointed out that
there were more girls than boys in the class and asked whether people
thought that girls would be more successful in general. This was still
the prevailing opinion, but the fact that there were a few waverers made
it possible to say, 'Well, let's find out.' So, following the same plan as
the last class, I had one boy and then one girl try it until we ran out
of boys. Once this activity started, the tone of the class completely
changed. It was fun, there was lots of cheering, and from the beginning
the activity took on a life of its own. Several girls could not do it, and
several boys could, so I said that I was not sure that science was on
my side today. In an aside to Johanna, who had been listening in while
she marked essays at her desk, I suggested that the effect of centre
of gravity might depend on puberty.

The possibility that they could overturn the official expectations,
combined with a boy–girl competition, made the activity lots of fun.
After 12 students had tried, the pattern I expected had begun to
emerge. I drew their attention to this, but Christine was unconvinced.
She asked me to try, and I was able to knock it over. Next, Johanna
tried and was not able to. One of the students picked up the puberty
aside I had made, so plainly the effect of puberty on my 'centre of
gravity' theory was in doubt. I asked people for a statement of the problem, and after several attempted explanations got, 'Why is it easier for
women to lean forward than men?' I also asked for guesses about the
cause of what we had seen, and got a range from the official centre of
gravity explanations to the more frivolous suggestion that girls had
longer necks and noses.

We then went on to an activity involving vinegar, raisins and baking soda. When the baking soda was added to a conical flask containing a few raisins, the raisins were supposed to float to the top. I had planned to distribute the materials carefully to avoid confusion, but in the excitement of the duster activity I forgot my plan. Instead of dividing the class into groups and naming the person to collect each piece of equipment, I found myself surrounded by a dozen students clamouring for vinegar, raisins, water, conical flasks, graduated cylinders and measuring spoons. Johanna saw my confusion and put aside her marking to help me. At this point, I called the rest of the students in and began a demonstration around the bench on which I had stored the materials.

The first time, I swished the flask around too enthusiastically and the foam created by the reaction between the baking soda and the vinegar poured out over my arm and the desk. The students (and Johanna) seemed to like this, and someone said: 'This is what I call science!' Only one of the raisins rose up on the cloud of gas, so I tried again with less agitation, and two of the three rose. With the class gathered around the bench, I asked what the problem was ('Why does the raisin rise when the baking soda and vinegar are added?'), and explained that the reason was that the reaction between them created bubbles of gas which attached to the raisins and lifted them to the surface. I asked people why they thought some raisins rose and others didn't and was offered a series of suggestions relating to size, weight and surface area. It was now time to clean up, so the group gathered around the bench broke up, washed the glassware and moved off to the morning meeting.

* * *

This story contains a series of practical teaching problems which were resolved spontaneously. When, for example, I was confronted by the class's surprising response to the duster activity – that they overwhelmingly thought that girls would be more successful – a series of possibilities flashed through my mind in a moment. Had they heard in the hallway from the other class? Did it matter if they had? What else could I do, anyway? I had no time to develop or consider alternative strategies, and I felt obliged by the pressure of my audience to move smoothly and confidently on to organizing the activity I had announced, so I put aside the uncomfortable possibility that some of the students already knew what was going to happen.

The second example of spontaneity in this story concerns my decision to abandon the small-group focus of the activity involving raisins and vinegar. Having lost my mental place in the lesson plan, and briefly overwhelmed by the press of students around my bench, I spontaneously called the remainder of the class in for a demonstration of the experiment. Had I been teaching a more difficult class this option would not have been open to me, but with 19 enthusiastic and biddable students and the possibility of additional assistance from Johanna, I was able to seize the moment and develop a better lesson than I had planned. And in the process I learned that with a class as small, involved and tractable as this one, demonstrations can be at least as effective as small group experiments.

The third and final example of spontaneous reflection led to one of the best moments in my term of science teaching at Community School. The students liked the theatre of the conical flask overflowing down my arm, and they were curious about why some raisins would not rise. Rather than participating in a lesson where the students guessed at the name of problem I had prepared, we framed a new problem from our observations and were left guessing at possible explanations. The genuine sense of enquiry raised by this unforeseen outcome was, I think, what the writers of the syllabus had in mind when they contributed their own tried and true lessons on problems, observations and inferences.

SUMMARY AND CONCLUSIONS

This chapter has outlined the range of reflection which emerged in our collaborative work. Reflection has been portrayed in terms of two dimensions: the forms and the interests of reflection. The two dimensions were proposed as complementary, in that each of the interests may be served by each of the forms of reflection, and examples were provided for each of the possible combinations of interest and form. Some others who have written about reflection have connected a single interest with a single form of reflection, for example Carr and Kemmis's critical interest and enquiry and Mezirow's critical interest and introspection. Other writers have connected a single interest with a range of forms: in Schon's case, various versions of his reflection-in-action and reflection-on-action were represented in all four of the forms of reflection, and are in each case associated with the problematic interest identified in this framework. In Johanna's work, however, some interests and forms were more prominent than others: in short, introspection was most often with a personal interest; replay and rehearsal, enquiry and spontaneity were overwhelmingly pursued with a problematic interest. There were a few examples where Johanna followed the critical interest through introspection, replay and rehearsal, and spontaneity, and there were even fewer examples which seemed to be informed by the technical interest in any form of reflection.

This framework of analysis emerged from the experience of the case study, and was not prepared until the empirical phase of the project had been completed. It was shaped by the intimate and introspective data available from a long-term, collaborative case study in which both the researcher and teacher were involved in reflecting on the experience of teaching. In addition, the framework was influenced by the preconceptions about teachers' knowledge and reflection I brought to the study, by the particular circumstances of the study, and by the relationship which Johanna and I developed. Because Johanna is such an open and forthcoming person, the introspective reflection tends to be personal. Because she is intuitive rather than rationalist, there was never any prospect that the study would document in detail the technical interest. Because Johanna sees herself as having reached a position of considerable freedom from external constraints in her teaching, she was unlikely to focus in great detail on the emancipatory interest of critical reflection. In a similar way, because I was more interested in how she and I solved the practical problems of the classroom than in reshaping the conditions of Johanna's work, it is not surprising that more attention was devoted to the problematic interest than to critique. In other studies, teachers and researchers working in different conditions and carrying forward different horizons of understanding about their lives and work might well engage in patterns of reflection which favour other of the interests and forms identified here. These are possibilities which others may choose to explore.

The value of a typology such as the forms and interests of reflection developed in this chapter is that it allows for a more subtle and textured account of teachers' reflection than either a Habermasian distinction between three interests or Schon's dichotomy alone can offer. The disadvantage of such typologies is that the effort to make the set of distinctions clear may lead to the impression that a particular typology is offered as the final word on the phenomena it describes. This is not the case with this conceptualization of reflection. The categories in this typology are neither as separate nor as exhaustive as they may appear when represented as 16 individual boxes on a chart. The categories on each dimension have been separated for the purpose of analysis; one interest of reflection may be dominant without the other interests being abandoned; and teachers may move from one form of reflection to another within a single conversation.

What remains to be explored in this study are the consequences of reflection: why did our reflection lead Johanna to the particular horizons of understanding which were described in Chapters 3 and 4? Thus far, the argument has focused on the individual choices made by Johanna, as if her choice were unconstrained. Men and women make their history, but not in circumstances of their own choosing. The final chapter, 'Continuity and Change', explores some of the ways in which the possibilities of Johanna's action were constrained by her repertoire, her biography, and by the traditions within which she works.

NOTES

1. A version of this argument also appears in Louden (1991).
2. See Habermas (1971), especially pp. 301–17. See also van Manen's (1977) theory of the practical in curriculum; McCutcheon's (1981) description of approaches to enquiry; Soltis's (1984) description of educational research; May and Zimpher's (1986) theoretical perspectives on supervision; Carr and Kemmis's (1986) work on educational theory and practice; and Grundy's (1987) description of forms of curriculum practice.
3. Although Habermas first offered his theory of knowledge-constitutive interests as 'quasi-transcendental', that is, as fundamental to the human condition in general, this claim has been the subject of a series of critiques concerning the possibility that such interests could transcend culture and language. See, for example, Bernstein (1985, pp. 13–21) and Held (1980, pp. 389–98). The issue at stake here, however, is not the transcendental status of such interests but their usefulness in explaining the range of

interests in reflection. For this reason, I have chosen to use Habermas's categories as a point of departure.

4. On Hunter and reflection, see the debate between Sergiovanni (1985, 1986) and Goldsberry (1986) in the *Journal of Curriculum and Supervision*.

5. See Cruickshank *et al*. (1981) for an account of this programme and Gore (1987) for a critical commentary.

6. Turner-Muecke, for instance, has provided a personal account of reflection-in-action in her own clinical supervision (Turner-Muecke *et al.*, 1986).

7. See, for example, van Manen (1977), Mezirow (1981), Berlack and Berlack (1981), Carr and Kemmis (1986) and Zeichner and Liston (1987).

8. The account by Bertola in Grundy (1987) is more quintessentially 'critical' than any of the examples available in the case study.

9. Here I am thinking of the difficulties which may be experienced in in-service education which touches people too closely (see Lewis and Simon, 1986, for a case in point), and school board–sponsored programme of peer or mentor supervision where pairs of teachers are chosen for reasons of administrative convenience rather than established trust between teachers (see Wallace, 1989).

10. This conceptualization of classroom environment is drawn from a literature review of the conditions of teachers' knowledge use by Huberman (1983).

11. Peer or micro teaching, such as Cruickshank *et al.'s* (1981) 'reflective teaching' is one example in initial teacher education, but it may be argued that such artificial situations have a difference that makes all the difference: they lack the press of 30 youngsters' conflicting preferences and intentions. A more convincing example from in-service education is role training based on Moreno's role theory, described in Williams *et al.* (1986).

12. See Munby and Russell (1989) for a review of Schon (1983, 1987) in which they make a similar comment of Shulman's notion of reflection.

Chapter 6

Continuity and Change

Over time, Johanna has developed an extensive repertoire of teaching: a set of standard patterns of teaching, familiar content and effective resolutions to common pedagogical problems. This repertoire involves a set of practical responses to the education–control dilemma: how can she help individual students learn in an environment which requires her to control the behaviour of the group? For a skilful and experienced teacher, such as Johanna, the education–control trade-off is almost invisible. She appears to be able to achieve order and group cohesion without dampening the possibilities for individual learning. These patterns, content and resolutions to the problem of education and control are not arbitrary, but are historically based in Johanna's biography and experience as a teacher. Overall her repertoire forms a predisposition to act in the future, what has been called her horizon of understanding.

This horizon is not static but is constantly in the process of formation. Confronted by new problems in teaching, Johanna struggles towards a fusion of horizons. She attempts to solve new problems in ways consistent with the understanding she brings to the problem, a process which leads in turn to new horizons of understanding about teaching. These new problems expose the education–control dilemma, and Johanna works to include new resolutions in her repertoire and to drive this dilemma back underground. For some problems, her current repertoire may gracefully be extended to include solutions for the new problems; in other cases this is more difficult, and uncomfortable trade-offs between education and control are necessary.

Through a range of forms and interests of reflection, Johanna is able to overcome gaps in her understanding, and her teaching grows and changes. Johanna's horizon of understanding however is not merely idiosyncratic and personal: much of her understanding is shared by other teachers who have learned to teach within similar traditions of teaching. This final chapter explores some of the ways in which tradition constrains Johanna's teaching and promotes continuity rather than change in her understanding and action.

TRADITIONS OF TEACHING

The advantage of case study research on teaching is that it fully elaborates the details which make so much difference to the meaning practitioners make of their work. The expansiveness of a case study allows the particulars of a teacher's practice to emerge in a fully elaborated context. By now, we know a great deal about the sorts of classroom pattern Johanna prefers, what she thinks is essential and peripheral in teaching, what would lead her to make changes, how she might go about making those changes, and what sorts of change would be easiest for her to make. These particulars have been shaped historically: by her biography; by the hopes and dreams she carries forward; by the patterns, content and resolutions to dilemmas of education and control in her standard repertoire of lessons; and by the reflection which took place during our collaborative work together.

One of the potential weaknesses of attempting to understand larger social processes such as educational change through case study research on individual teachers is that the concentration on these particulars may seem to imply that Johanna's repertoire and her predispositions to understanding and action are entirely a matter of individual choice. Certainly she had to construct her particular ways of understanding and action through many years of personal effort and several sharp mid-career changes which were outside her control, but her present horizon of understanding has much in common with the horizons of teachers she has never met. With these teachers, she shares several *traditions* of teaching: common ways of understanding content, pedagogy, students and the social milieu of schooling. Such similarities between teachers have been described in a variety of theoretical terms, including ideology (Sharp and Green, 1975; King, 1978), culture (Waller, 1932; Jackson, 1968; Lortie, 1975), cultures (Feiman-Nemser and Floden, 1986) and tradition (Blyth, 1965). These similarities are also suggested by a series of descriptive terms which seem appropriate to Johanna: progressive teachers (Central Advisory Council, 1967), interpretation teachers (Barnes, 1976), developmental teachers (Hargreaves, 1986), and teachers using an invisible pedagogy

(Bernstein, 1980). More than this, scholars have drawn attention to similarities among art teachers (Bennet, 1985), English teachers (St John Brooks, 1983), teachers in primary schools (Bennett, 1976), middle schools (Hargreaves, 1986) and alternative schools (Levin, 1984), all of which resonate with what we have seen of Johanna's teaching. Whichever conceptual apparatus or labels may be preferred, it is clear that Johanna is more progressive than traditional, more familiar with the arts than with academic disciplines, more a generalist than a specialist, and more an alternative than a mainstream teacher.

Rather than rehearse the now familiar particulars of Johanna's teaching in the context of each of these terms, labels and areas of specialism, we may consider the startling similarity between what we now know of Johanna and the following comment by a music teacher in a middle school in the West Riding of Yorkshire. Music, Mrs Weaver said:

> is one of those areas, as art is, where your communion
> with children is very close. And it's an emotional subject
> as English is and art can be. You've got to *talk* your
> feelings and I think this is where communication comes in
> because as soon as you're communicating in that way
> with a child, they start giving back and this carries on to
> when they are doing other things. Sort of rapport is still
> there because it carries from that area. I think that
> anybody who teaches in the creative arts has this with
> the kids because it's emotionally based ... whereas if you
> are dealing with a factual subject, a scientific subject,
> you're dealing more with objects and reactions. Actually
> how you *feel* about SO_2 coming out of a bottle doesn't
> come into it, you know.

(Hargreaves, 1986, p. 188)

Like Johanna, Mrs Weaver was in mid-career, had taught a variety of age ranges, in formal and informal contexts, was a music specialist with generalist interests in middle schools, was more interested in communication than in content, and was dismissive of the emotionally bare and factual approach she associated with teaching

187

science. Although these two women were separated by thousands of miles and their own quite different biographies and careers, these words could easily have been Johanna's. This comment by Mrs Weaver captures Johanna's attitude towards content in education, and the following comment about the work of Mrs Bell, an Australian English teacher, echoes her attitudes towards students' independence:

> Mrs Bell has evolved over many years a very clear stance
> on the power of student intention as opposed to student
> coercion. She admits that she could have forced the class
> to be more superficially efficient in getting through
> the work. She could also have imposed a tighter,
> less-negotiable structure. Instead she provided firm
> parameters within which she negotiated groupings, task
> allocations, and the form and content of assignments.
> She kept throwing the responsibility of choice and
> time-management back on the class. The result was
> a sequence where the class was slow to begin and
> floundering for a week or so. Gradually, as intentions and
> ownership took hold, the momentum gathered until in
> many ways the class took over.

(Boomer, 1987, p. 10)

Johanna, like Mrs Bell, is committed to the power of students' intention, provides clear parameters for their action, negotiates with students even when it would be more superficially simple to use her authority, and consequently provides opportunities for students to take charge of their own learning.

Like Mrs Bell, my own background is in a particular variant of progressivism called 'growth model' English (Dixon, 1975), a tradition that has many points of contact with Johanna's progressive, art and music, middle-school generalist traditions. As Chapter 1 shows, membership of the same traditions of teaching was an essential part of our agreement to work together. On the day I first met her, the comment I made about the relationship between students' emotional states and their learning and Johanna's reaction (that they were 'the same thing') suggested that we shared a broadly progressive tradition. During the following few weeks, as we circled around one another, we continued to explore the similarities between us. Before Johanna finally agreed to participate in the study she formally interviewed me because she wanted to be sure we shared some of the same values about teaching. As the study proceeded, we realized that not only did we share similar hopes and dreams for schooling but we also had something to teach each other about achieving our goals in the classroom. Membership of the same traditions provided us with grounds for intersubjective agreement: Johanna and I shared similar attitudes to content, to independence, to the importance of encouragement, to the need for structure to support learning, and to the importance of students' emotional safety if they were to take the risk of learning. Intersubjective agreement is a powerful force for continuity in teachers' work. People who agree on the meaning of classroom events and on the grounds for judging whether teaching is done well or poorly find it easier to agree what should be done next. Such tacit or explicit agreements of people working within the same traditions of teaching both enable and constrain the growth of understanding, as the next section suggests.

THE POWER OF TRADITION

One way to think of traditions is in terms of shared traditions of teaching: a progressive tradition, an alternative school tradition, a middle-school/generalist tradition. More than these generalized notions of intersubjective agreement from one school to another, traditions may also be thought of as the highly specific and taken-for-granted meanings and practices which exist within any particular social setting. These sedimented meaning structures exert a powerful force on the limits of teachers' possible actions.

Johanna left Prince Alfred School because she no longer had the energy to resist the academic tradition of the school. What attracted her to Community School was that she liked the people and expected that her ways of teaching would be more appreciated there. The teachers, parents and students were all members of the artistic-professional milieu which supports and populates alternative schools and of which Johanna herself is a member. Here, she thought, was a school where she would have the freedom to teach as she had always wanted to teach. In many ways this was the case. At Community School there is a genuine sense of community, a warm and caring

189

environment, and respect for artistic activities. However, her freedom to teach as she wants to teach is in some ways constrained by the power of tradition at Community School.

In her first year at the school Johanna was often troubled by the lack of structure, what she called the 'craziness' of the school, and in her second year she found that there was more room to move in changing some of the traditions that bothered her. She was now an established member of the staff, and Bob, the custodian of the tradition of Community School, had moved on to another school. Johanna's colleagues, Miles and Freida, were willing to make some changes in order to please Johanna and for the benefit of the school. They discussed the scheduling of the afternoons, reduced the amount of 'independent time', postponed the introduction of independent field trips, and had reorganized the school's physical space so that it would be easier to keep tidy.

Despite these agreements, intended to make the school more orderly and predictable, Johanna continued to be at odds with some of the traditions of the school. In particular, she continued to be troubled by lack of punctuality, untidiness and what she once called the 'depths of despair' theory of alternative education which sometimes seemed to be operating in the school. She could minimize the impact of these issues by teaching in a separate classroom with a door, through routines which encouraged tidiness and punctuality, and by providing a clear structure within which students could learn to take more responsibility for their own learning. What she could not do, however, was control the power of the living tradition outside her classroom. As long as I was involved in Community School, I continued to see Johanna struggle with the consequences of the rest of the school's use of space and time in the open-area classrooms. Students, especially the Grade 8s, were always late after break, were always looking for opportunities to leave the confines of her class for the wide open spaces of the other classrooms, and chafed against her expectations of standards for finished work. This mismatch between Johanna's particular variety of the progressive tradition and the living traditions of Community School continued to provide an agenda for her reflection throughout the study. In 'Writing' and 'Science', Chapters 3 and 4, several of the dilemmas of education and control we faced were informed by Johanna's struggle to lead students towards a sufficiently orderly and safe environment to support the kind of independent education Community School prides itself on offering but does not always achieve. So, although Community School opens the possibilities for Johanna to achieve her hopes and dreams, the power of tradition is also a material constraint on her action.

REFLECTION AND TRADITION

The essential condition for reflection is some gap in understanding, some difference which must be overcome. Johanna knew, for example, that students needed to write more carefully and correctly, but she did not know how to help them; she knew that the Grade 8 class was producing substandard work on the illustrated book project but did not know how to insist on standards without discouraging some of the less able students; she knew that I was trying to help by teaching from the science syllabus but she also knew how uncomfortable she would be trying to teach such school science; she had a sense that classification was essential to biological knowledge and she stumbled across a clearer understanding of the reasons why it was important as she taught a series of three classes; I lost my place in a science lesson on 'problems', used my spontaneity to overcome the gap, and learned the value of demonstrations in science. Each of these acts of reflection occurred within our separate horizons of understanding and our partly shared traditions of teaching. The act of reflection consists of attempting to overcome a gap in understanding using the preconceptions one presently has. The result of reflection is that almost imperceptible growth in understanding which has been called fusion of horizons.

Fusion of horizons, however, occurs in relation to established traditions as well as personal horizons of understanding. Traditions supply a person with a language and a way of seeing the world, and it is this intersubjective framework that limits the power of reflection. It is not that a tradition and one's present horizons allow no room for growth and change, but that reflection is a matter of 'invention within limits', to use Bourdieu's phrase (Bourdieu, 1977). Even reaching understandings similar to other teachers in the same tradition requires an arduous process of construction of meaning.

Reflection allows people to explore the limits of invention and to transcend the tradition and horizons within which reflection takes place. The larger the gap, the more creative the invention needs to be, as Johanna's varied career shows. When pressed to transform herself from a progressive primary teacher in the South Bronx to a specialist middle-school teacher in London, Johanna was able to bridge the gap and during that five years of teaching reinvented herself as an art specialist. When her emigration to Canada forced her back to teaching as a generalist in a primary school Johanna had serious difficulties adjusting and – propelled by changes in industrial conditions – instead reinvented herself as a specialist music teacher. This was a difficult and painful experience and she took the earliest opportunity to return to teaching art. There she was able to expand further her specialist skills to include drama teaching. When, finally, she felt that her efforts were not being recognized by teachers with a more academic focus she transferred to Community School. All of these changes required Johanna to bridge the gap between the old and the new, between her horizons of understanding, traditions of teaching and the new experiences which confronted her. Sometimes the gaps were small, for example expanding her skills into drama, and other times the gaps were large, such as when she learned to be a music specialist. In the latter case the gap could only be bridged by Johanna recognizing that she would never be the 'minor scales' music teacher her instructors had tried to make her.

In the changes Johanna made in 'Writing' the gap in understanding was small. The changes were not only consistent with her patterns of teaching and her hopes and dreams, but also with Community School's broadly progressive and alternative traditions. In the new context of a process approach to the teaching of writing there were new dilemmas of education and control to be resolved, but the resolutions we found were compatible with Community School traditions and with her own patterns of teaching. We resolved the productivity problem in the Grade 8 class, for example, by using a familiar problem-solving class discussion pattern, and by dividing the class into more and less independent groups, just as Miles, Bob and Freida had done in the years before Johanna arrived at the school.

When we came to bridge the gap between our present horizons and the science syllabus, we used the same range of reflection: connecting what was happening with our biographies and experience, rehearsing our plans and our successes and failures, making mid-course corrections on the basis of our enquiry into the problems we encountered, and capitalizing on a few spontaneous inventions. Notwithstanding this full range of reflection, we never really bridged the gap between our horizons and the tradition of school science teaching. I began by attempting to submit to the tradition of school science, to follow the patterns of teaching and the content of the guidelines. This was not easy for me, because I lacked both the background knowledge and the experience of the sort of structured and careful lesson planning required to manage the safe and effective use of science equipment. For perhaps two different reasons, I was willing to submit to the tradition of the subject. The first was pragmatic: I was more concerned to be helpful to Johanna than I was with students' learning, and the second was my lack of conviction that it would do students any harm for them to learn a little school science, no matter how irrelevant it seemed to be. In addition, I had the advantage of a (slightly) stronger content background than Johanna which made it possible for me to convince the students that I was indeed a real science teacher.

For Johanna, my willingness to submit to the tradition of school science conflicted with her personal notions of what constituted valuable education. It required attitudes towards factual content she did not have, particular content knowledge she did not have, and patterns of teaching she did not have. In short, the gap between her horizons and the tradition was too great to be bridged by our reflection. We canvassed the possibilities of three approaches: the content-centred approach I began with, the individual progress approach of the colleague we visited before the start of the school year, and the discovery approach she had previously seen in action in alternative schools. None of these versions of school science seemed educationally worth while to Johanna. Unlike our experience in 'Writing', where the goal of reflection was to bridge a gap within two compatible traditions of teaching, here the gap was between two conflicting traditions: between the arts and science (Snow, 1964), between romantic and rationalist cultures (St John Brooks, 1983), and between developmental and academic cultures of teaching (Hargreaves, 1986).

Consequently, our reflection was devoted to finding ways of dealing with science which were within our established patterns of teaching and horizons of understanding. Rather than bridging the gap between the two traditions, we found ways of turning an alien tradition into a familiar tradition. Towards this end, Johanna contributed an established pattern of research assignments and I contributed some demonstration lessons carried forward from my days as an English teacher. The result was a series of lessons which paid more attention to a goal we were interested in pursuing, helping students become more independent learners, than to teaching the science content of the guidelines. In all of our reflection, in all of its forms and interests, Johanna never seriously considered the possibility that she ought to submit to the tradition of school science embodied in the syllabus.[1] Instead of expanding our horizons to include school science, our response was to bridge the gap of understanding by changing science into something we could understand.

THE POSSIBILITY OF CHANGE

In the analysis of this case study evidence I have argued that the tacit, context-specific and biographically embedded nature of Johanna's personal understanding of teaching and the power of tradition shape and limit her capacity to change her teaching. The changes she did make, however, were made in the context of a carefully developed collaborative partnership.[2]

Our partnership was founded on similar traditions of teaching and hopes and dreams for education, similarities which allowed substantial intersubjective agreement about the meaning of classroom events. Despite the similarities, there were enough differences to create opportunities for each of us to help the other across gaps of understanding. Unlike many working relationships between a practising teacher and an outsider (teacher–consultant; teacher–principal; teacher–researcher) there was no hierarchical difference between us. Our roles were different but equal. Although it transpired that Johanna sometimes adopted the attitude of the researcher and I eventually 'went native' as a teacher, there was never any doubt that she was the master teacher and I was the researcher interested in her work. As a temporary resident of Canada, separated from my own past and future, I had no stake in projecting an image as an expert teacher, researcher or consultant. I was able to be as humble as I truly felt about what I had to offer Johanna. This might not have been the case if I had been a school board officer or university researcher with a career to protect, or if I had been working in the school system in my own home town.

Throughout our work together we shared both the workload and the risk of participating in such an intensive and personal case study. When I arrived at the school I offered to help out in any way I could, and I meant it. I was indifferent to whether helping meant grading papers, teaching lessons or washing Johanna's car. As the study developed, and Johanna and I became immersed in solving the problems of teaching writing and science, I may have cost her more time and effort than I saved, but I was still able to make a real difference on several occasions of short-handedness and crisis. By working alongside Johanna I also shared the risks of participation. She took the risk that I was documenting her 'mistakes', and I took the risk of demonstrating my own inadequacy as a teacher as I attempted to recover teaching skills I had not practised for five years and learned to teach an unfamiliar subject.

The trust we developed was quite personal in character. We found that we liked each other, we became friends and the project became more than a piece of work for us both. I enjoyed working with Johanna and participating in the life of the school; she liked having me around and hoped my research would go well. Fortunately, our collaboration was not constrained by a preordained research agenda. I was committed to completing a case study research project and I thought that the study might explore a teacher's taken-for-granted understanding of teaching and the ways that understanding changes, but I was not committed to a particular idea or framework. Had there been less to say about reflection, the study might have had more to say about routines and habits, for example.

As our collaboration proceeded it became plain that our partnership increased Johanna's opportunities for reflection. Because I spent so much time with her and asked so many questions, Johanna had more reason to connect her biography with her experience in the form of reflection I have called *introspection*, to make sense of her experience of teaching through *replay and rehearsal*, to find time for *enquiry* into problems she faced, and to be aware of the effects of her *spontaneity* on the growth in her knowledge of teaching. Without the presence of a colleague in her classroom she would not have had an audience for all this reflection, and the range of reflection might have been more limited. She would no doubt have rehearsed some of her problems in the staffroom with Miles and Freida, but it seems less likely that she would have continued to worry about the texts of the students' illustrated books, to have canvassed so wide a range of options in science, or to have thought so much about her biography, her repertoire and her hopes and dreams.

Our collaboration may have had less influence on the *interests* than on *forms* of reflection in the study. Our intersubjective agreement about what constituted a problem in teaching meant that we moved quickly to discussing how we might resolve problems. Had Johanna or I been more personally inclined towards a critical interest, or had we been working in a school which more powerfully constrained her action, our problem-solving might have been framed by more critical reflection. In similar ways, one may imagine collaborative enquiry more interested in technique, or in personal growth.

Whatever the forms and interests of reflection may be in other cases, this case study suggests that collaborative enquiry has an important role to play in educational change. Whereas externally mandated curriculum reform has failed to produce lasting changes in classrooms, collaborative enquiry between teachers, and between teachers and researchers, holds the possibility for gradual and lasting educational change. For most of my time at Community School my daily work was as a collaborating teacher, someone for Johanna to talk to and for her to watch struggling with the same problems she faced in her own teaching. Her colleagues at Community School provided an unusually caring and supportive environment, but they did not have as much of what I had to offer – *time*: time to listen, time to watch, time to help out, and time to act in Johanna's place while she watched me.

In the time we had, we made some progress on the most accessible problems and less progress on problems which required us to submit to unfamiliar traditions of teaching. The progress we made, however, was genuine. It was not a matter of one-off lessons to demonstrate 'active learning' to a supervisor, or of grudging adherence to externally mandated changes. If there is a single lesson to be drawn from this single case study, it is that serious educational change at Johanna's classroom level proceeded slowly, by the gradual fusion of her horizons rather than by sudden leaps of insight. The changes she did make were deeply connected to her biography, her repertoire and her hopes and dreams for education. Administrators and academics, working outside the classroom and animated by political and intellectual agendas for change, may hope for a simpler and more sudden process of change. Too often, however, they express their hopes for change in programmes and imperatives that teachers experience as arbitrary or wrong-headed. Collaborative enquiry offers a slower, more generous and more powerful path towards educational change, and impels those outside schools who hope for change to approach teachers with respect. Proposals for change in teachers' practice are proposals to change teachers' lives, and should be approached with care and humility, not arrogance and certainty.

NOTES

1. This is a familiar problem in the literature on innovation in science, albeit in the context of experienced teachers of school science rejecting the innovative approaches of the Schools Council Integrated Science Project (Olson, 1981) and the Australian Science Education Project (Fraser, 1978).
2. University-based researchers have often argued that teachers and researchers ought to develop more collaborative relationships in order to improve the quality of both research and teaching. See, for example, Stenhouse (1983), Rudduck (1975), Carr and Kemmis (1986), Tripp (1987) Connelly and Clandinin (1988).

Bibliography

Barnes, D. (1976) *From Communication to Curriculum.* Harmondsworth: Penguin.

Bennet, C. (1985) 'Paint, pots or promotion: art teachers' attitudes towards their careers,' in S. Ball and I. Goodson (eds) *Teachers' Lives and Careers.* Lewes: Falmer Press.

Bennett, S. N. (1976) *Teaching Styles and Pupil Progress.* London: Open Books.

Berlack, A. and Berlack, H. (1981) *Dilemmas of Teaching.* New York: Methuen.

Bernstein, B. (1980) 'Class and pedagogies: visible and invisible,' in W. B. Dockrell and D. Hamilton (eds) *Rethinking Educational Research.* London: Hodder and Stoughton.

Bernstein, R. J. (1985) *Habermas and Modernity.* Cambridge, MA: MIT Press.

Blyth, W. A. L. (1965) *English Primary Education: A Sociological Description* – Vol. II: *Background.* London: Routledge and Kegan Paul.

Boomer, G. (1987.) *Changing Education: Reflections on National Issues in Education in Australia.* Canberra: Commonwealth Schools Commission.

Bourdieu, P. (1977) *Outline of a Theory of Practice.* Cambridge: Cambridge University Press.

Boyd, E. and Fales, A. (1983) 'Reflective learning: key to learning from experience,' *Journal of Humanistic Psychology,* 23 (2): 99–117.

Butt, R. L. and Raymond, D. (1987) 'Arguments for using qualitative approaches in understanding teacher thinking: the case for biography,' *Journal of Curriculum Studies,* 7 (1): 62–93.

Carr, W. and Kemmis, S. (1986) *Becoming Critical: Education,*

Knowledge and Action Research. Lewes: Falmer Press.

Central Advisory Council for Education in England (1967) *Children and their Primary Schools*, 2 vols. London: HMSO. (The Plowden Report)

Clandinin, D. J. and Connelly, F. M. (1986) 'Rhythms in teaching: the narrative study of teachers' personal practical knowledge of classrooms,' *Teaching and Teacher Education*, 2 (4): 377–87.

Clark, W. and Peterson, P. (1986) 'Teachers' thought processes,' in M. C. Wittrock (ed.) *Handbook of Research on Teaching*. New York: Macmillan.

Cole, A. (1987) 'Teachers' spontaneous adaptations: a mutual interpretation,' PhD thesis, University of Toronto.

Connelly, F. M. and Clandinin, D. J. (1986a) 'The reflective practitioner and practitioners' narrative unities,' *Canadian Journal of Education*, 11 (2): 184–99.

Connelly, F. M. and Clandinin, D. J. (1986b) 'On narrative method, personal philosophy, and narrative unities in the story of teaching,' *Journal of Research in Science Teaching*, 23 (4): 293–310.

Connelly, F. M. and Clandinin, D. J. (1987) 'On narrative method, biography and narrative unities in the study of teaching,' *Journal of Educational Thought*, 21 (3): 130–9.

Connelly, F. M. and Clandinin, D. J. (1988) *Teachers as Curriculum Planners: Narratives of Experience.* Toronto: OISE Press; New York: Teachers College Press.

Cruickshank, D. R., Kennedy, J. J., Williams, E. J., Holton, J. and Fay, D. E. (1981) 'Evaluation of reflective teaching outcomes,' *Journal of Educational Research*, 75 (1): 26–32.

Dewey, J. (1933) *How We Think*. Boston: Heath.

Dixon, J. (1975) *Growth through English*, 3rd edn. London: Oxford University Press.

Elbaz, F. L. (1983) *Teacher Thinking: A Study of Practical Knowledge*. London: Croom Helm.

Feiman-Nemser, S. and Floden, R. E. (1986) 'The cultures of teaching,' in M. C. Wittrock (ed.) *Handbook of Research on Teaching*. New York: Macmillan.

Fraser, B. (1978) 'Australian Science Education Project: overview of evaluation studies,' *Science Education*, 62 (3): 417–26.

Fullan, M. (1982) *The Meaning of Educational Change*. Toronto: OISE Press; New York: Teachers College Press.

Gadamer, H-G. (1975) *Truth and Method*, trans. and ed. G. Barden and J. Cumming. New York: Seabury Press.

Gadamer, H-G. (1976) *Philosophical Hermeneutics*, trans. D. E. Linge. Berkeley: University of California Press.

Goldsberry, L. E. (1986) 'The reflective mindscape,' *Journal of Curriculum and Supervision*, 1 (4): 347–52.

Gordon, T. (1970) *Parent Effectiveness Training: The 'No-lose' Program for Raising Responsible Children*. New York: P. H. Wyden.

Gordon, T. (1974) *TET: Teacher Effectiveness Training*. New York: P. H. Wyden.

Gore, J. (1987) 'Reflecting on reflective teaching,' *Journal of Teacher Education*, 38 (2): 33–9.

Gramsci, A. (1971) *Prison Notebooks*, trans. Q. Hoare and G. Nowell-Smith. London: Lawrence and Wishart.

Graves, D. (1983) *Writing: Teachers and Children at Work*. London: Heinemann.

Grundy, S. (1987) *Curriculum: Product or Praxis*. Lewes: Falmer Press.

Habermas, J. (1971) *Knowledge and Human Interests*, trans. J. Shapiro. Boston: Beacon Press.

Hargreaves, A. (1986) *Two Cultures of Schooling: The Case of Middle Schools*. Lewes: Falmer Press.

Held, D. (1980) *Introduction to Critical Theory*. Berkeley and Los Angeles: University of California Press.

Huberman, M. (1983) 'Recipes for busy kitchens: a situational analysis of routine knowledge use in schools,' *Knowledge: Creation, Diffusion, Utilization*, 4: 478–510.

Huberman, M. and Miles, M. (1984) *Innovation Up Close: How School Improvement Works*. New York: Plenum.

Hunt, D. E. (1976) 'Teachers' adaptation: "reading" and "flexing" to students,' *Journal of Teacher Education*, 27: 268–75.

Hunter, M. (1983) *Mastery Teaching*. El Segundo, CA: Tip Publications.

Jackson, P. W. (1968) *Life in Classrooms*. New York: Holt, Rinehart and Winston.

King, R. (1978) *All Things Bright and Beautiful? A Sociological*

Study of Infants' Classrooms. Chichester: John Wiley.

Kirst, M. W. and Meister, G. R. (1985) 'Turbulence in American secondary schools: what reforms last?,' *Curriculum Inquiry*, 15 (2): 169–86.

Lampert, M. (1984) 'Teaching about thinking and thinking about teaching,' *Journal of Curriculum Studies*, 16: 1–16.

Laurence, M. (1974) *The Diviners*. Toronto: McClelland and Stewart.

Leinhardt, G. *et al*. (1987) 'Introduction and integration of classroom routines by expert teachers,' *Curriculum Inquiry*, 17 (2): 135–76.

Levin, M. A. (1984) 'What's "alternative" about Toronto's alternative schools?,' unpublished paper, Ontario Institute for Studies in Education.

Lewis, M. and Simon, R. (1986) 'A discourse not intended for her: learning and teaching within patriarchy,' *Harvard Educational Review*, 56 (4): 457–72.

Lortie, D. C. (1975) *Schoolteacher: A Sociological Study*. Chicago: University of Chicago Press.

Louden, W. (1989) 'Understanding teaching: meaning and method in collaborative research,' PhD thesis, University of Toronto.

Louden, W. (1991) 'Reflection and the development of teachers' knowledge,' in A. Hargreaves and M. Fullan (eds) *Understanding Teacher Education*. London: Cassell.

McCutcheon, G. (1981) 'On the interpretation of classroom observations,' *Educational Researcher*, 10 (5): 5–10.

May, W. T. and Zimpher, N. L. (1986) 'An examination of three theoretical perspectives on supervision: perceptions of preservice field supervision,' *Journal of Curriculum and Supervision*, 1 (2): 83–99.

Mezirow, J. (1981) 'A critical theory of adult learning and education,' *Adult Education*, 32 (1): 3–24.

Miles, M. B. and Huberman, A. M. (1984) 'Drawing valid meaning from qualitative data: toward a shared craft,' *Educational Researcher*, 13 (5): 20–30.

Munby, H. and Russell, T. (1989) 'Educating the reflective teacher: an essay review of two books by Donald Schon,' *Journal of Curriculum Studies*, 21 (1): 71–80.

Nolan, J. F. and Huber, T. (1989) 'Nurturing the reflective

practitioner through instructional supervision: a review of the literature,' *Journal of Curriculum and Supervision*, 4 (2): 126–45.

Olson, J. K. (1981) 'Teacher influence in the classroom: a context for understanding curriculum translation,' *Instructional Science*, 10: 259–75.

Olson, J. K. (1985) 'Changing our ideas about change,' *Canadian Journal of Education*, 10 (3): 294–308.

Ontario (1987) Intermediate English Curriculum Guideline. Toronto: Ministry of Eduction.

Rudduck, J. (1975) 'Teacher research and research based teacher education,' *Journal of Education for Teaching*, 11 (3): 281–9.

St John Brooks, C. (1983) 'English: a curriculum for personal development?,' in M. Hammersley and A. Hargreaves (eds), *Curriculum Practice: Some Sociological Case Studies*. Lewes: Falmer Press.

Schon, D. A. (1983) *The Reflective Practitioner*. New York: Basic Books.

Schon, D. A. (1987) *Educating the Reflective Practitioner*. San Francisco, CA: Jossey-Bass.

Schutz, A. and Luckmann, T. (1973) *The Structures of the Lifeworld*. Evanston, IL: Northwestern University Press.

Sergiovanni, T. J. (1985) 'Landscapes, mindscapes, and reflective practice in supervision,' *Journal of Curriculum and Supervision*, 1 (1): 5–17.

Sergiovanni, T. J. (1986) 'Understanding reflective practice,' *Journal of Curriculum and Supervision*, 1 (4): 353–9.

Sharp, R. and Green, S. (1975) *Education and Social Control: A Study in Progressive Education*. London: Routledge and Kegan Paul.

Shulman, L. (1986) 'Those who understand: foundations of the new reform,' *Harvard Educational Review*, 57 (1): 1–22.

Shulman, L. S. (1987) 'Knowledge and teaching: foundations of the new reform,' *Harvard Educational Review*, 57 (1): 1–22.

Snow, C. P. (1964) *The Two Cultures: And a Second Look*, 2nd edn. Cambridge: Cambridge University Press.

Soltis, J. F. (1984) 'On the nature of educational research,' *Educational Researcher*, 13 (10): 5–10.

Stenhouse, L. (1983) *Authority, Education and Emancipation.* London: Heinemann.

Tripp, D. H. (1987) 'Teachers, journals and collaborative research,' in W. J. Smyth, *Educating Teachers*. Lewes: Falmer Press.

Turner-Muecke, L. A., Russell, T. and Bowyer, J. (1986) 'Reflection-in-action: case study of a clinical supervisor,' *Journal of Curriculum and Supervision*, 2 (1): 40–9.

Van Manen, M. (1977) 'Linking ways of knowing with ways of being practical,' *Curriculum Inquiry*, 6 (2): 205–28.

Wallace, J. W. (1989) 'Personal–professional growth: self, situation and teacher image,' PhD thesis, University of Toronto.

Waller, W. (1932) *The Sociology of Teaching*. New York: John Wiley.

Weinsheimer, J. C. (1985) *Gadamer's Hermeneutics: A Reading of Truth and Method.* New Haven and London: Yale University Press.

Williams, P. A, Colliver, R. and Simpson, A. (1986) *Excellence in Teaching: Lessons from the Classroom Relationships Project.* Perth: Education Department of Western Australia.

Yinger, R. (1979) 'Routines in teacher planning,' *Theory in Practice*, 18: 163–9.

Zeichner, K. M. and Liston, D. P. (1987) 'Teaching student teachers to reflect,' *Harvard Educational Review*, 57 (1): 23–48.

Index

0146177

S. 2. £16.99.

JH
LOPMENT (Lou)

argreaves

DING TEACHING

This book is due for return on or before t⊢

HAROLD BRIDGES LIBRARY
S. MARTIN'S COLLEGE
LANCASTER

p 7066982